¹¹ The Lord said, "Go out and stand on the mountain in the presence of the Lord, for the Lord is about to pass by."

Then a great and powerful wind tore the mountains apart and shattered the rocks before the Lord, but the Lord was not in the wind. After the wind there was an earthquake, but the Lord was not in the earthquake. ¹² After the earthquake came a fire, but the Lord was not in the fire. And after the fire came a gentle whisper. ¹³ When Elijah heard it, he pulled his cloak over his face and went out and stood at the mouth of the cave.

Then a voice said to him, "What are you doing here, Elijah?"

I Kings 19:11-13 (NIV)

Understanding Your Call

*Observing God's call through the
eyes of 11 Biblical figures*

Abraham, Amos,

David, Esther, Jonah, Joseph,

Mary (Mother of Jesus),

Naaman's Servant Girl,

Philip, Rahab, & Samuel

Kevin Slimp, Editor

Contributors

Julie Blackwelder Holly, Wil Cantrell, Rob Couch, Bishop Robert Farr,
Aleze Fulbright, Phil Maynard, Larry Ousley,
Jacob Reedy, Kevin Slimp, & Bishop Debbie Wallace-Padgett

Market
Square
BOOKS

Understanding Your Call

Observing God's call through the eyes of 11 Biblical figures

©2018 Market Square Publishing Company, LLC.
books@marketsquarebooks.com
P.O. Box 23664   Knoxville, Tennessee 37933

ISBN: 978-0-9987546-6-6

Library of Congress: 2017919007

Printed and Bound in the United States of America

Cover Illustration & Book Design ©2018 Market Square Publishing, LLC
by Kevin Slimp

Editor: Kevin Slimp

Table of Contents

1. Samuel: A Voice in the Dark 3

2. Amos: Man of the Cloth 17

3. Rahab: Fulfilling Her Call 25

4. David: A Man After God's Own Heart 33

5. Joseph: An Interpreter of Dreams 43

6. Abraham: Listening to Outside Voices 55

7. Servant Girl: Called By God 65

8. Philip: Helping People Discover Jesus 75

9. Esther: A Jewish Queen 83

10. Mary: Mary Said Yes 91

11. Jonah: He Knew God's Voice 99

About the Authors 109

Introduction

Following our decision to create a book in honor of Larry Ousley, retired director of the Intentional Growth Center, the folks at Market Square Publishing invited a group of 10 United Methodist leaders to share their stories based on Biblical figures who answered their calls.

It is our prayer that study groups and Sunday School classes will find *Understanding Your Call* an effective resource for understanding how Biblical figures understood their calls from God in ways that might help readers better understand their own calls.

The proceeds from this book will be donated to the Intentional Growth Center, a ministry of the United Methodist Church, with offices at Lake Junaluska, North Carolina. These 10 writers have donated their work to create the book you are holding.

For me, this book has been a labor of love, offering the opportunity to meet a marvelous group of writers and to re-ignite a few friendships from decades ago. My hope is the spirit of each reader will be re-ignited by the words to follow.

Kevin Slimp, Editor

CHAPTER ONE

Samuel: A Voice in the Darkness

by Wil Cantrell

Out of Chaos, Order

> [5] And he ran to Eli and said, "Here I am; you called me."
> But Eli said, "I did not call; go back and lie down." So he went and lay down.
> [6] Again the Lord called, "Samuel!" And Samuel got up and went to Eli and said, "Here I am; you called me."
> "My son," Eli said, "I did not call; go back and lie down."
> [7] Now Samuel did not yet know the Lord: The word of the Lord had not yet been revealed to him.
> [8] A third time the Lord called, "Samuel!" And Samuel got up and went to Eli and said, "Here I am; you called me."
> Then Eli realized that the Lord was calling the boy.
> [9] So Eli told Samuel, "Go and lie down, and if he calls you, say, 'Speak, Lord, for your servant is listening.'" So Samuel went and lay down in his place.
>
> 1 Samuel 3:5-9 (NIV)

Primer

As you begin this chapter, take a moment to consider the following questions:

Have you ever heard God calling you?

If you have, was it in a still, small voice or in an overwhelming way?

In what ways do you listen for God's call?

In creation, God brought order out of chaos. God's call in our lives often brings order and clarity to what was previously chaos and confusion. This was true for the prophet Samuel and it is true for us.

Samuel's early life was filled with contradictions. His mother, Hannah, wanted a child so desperately that the intensity of her prayers was mistaken for the wailing of a drunk. When God granted her passionate plea to bear a son, she responded by leaving her child, Samuel, to be raised by the priests at the temple as soon as he was old enough to be weaned. As Samuel pondered his identity, he must have struggled to make sense of a mother who wanted him so badly, yet was willing to give him up so quickly.

While Samuel might have taken solace in the fact that his mother gave him up to pursue the most honorable of professions as a priest, whenever he looked around at the priests in charge of the temple, he saw very little that was honorable. Eli, the high priest, lacked the will to adequately discipline his adult children. Instead, he allowed his sons to intimidate the worshipers who came to sacrifice to God and become wealthy themselves by stealing the offerings. Samuel might have learned the ways of God from the teachings of the priests, but he assuredly learned the ways of sin by observing their actions. To this young man trying to find his way in a confusing world, God spoke in the middle of the night.

When God first called Samuel, he thought it was Eli calling him. Three times Samuel responded to the call by rushing to Eli's bedside only to be informed that Eli had not called him. Having grown up in the temple, we might think Samuel would know enough to wonder if perhaps it was God calling him instead of Eli. However, at this point in his life, the scriptures tell us that Samuel had never before felt God's presence and knew little of God (1 Samuel 3:7).

Finally, after being woken from sleep three times by Samuel, Eli sensed that God may be talking to Samuel. So, Eli instructed him to respond if he heard the call again by saying, "Speak, Lord, for your servant is listening (1 Samuel 3:10)." Samuel takes Eli's advice and when God calls a fourth time, Samuel finds himself in a conversation that will bring clarity to his life's purpose and alter the course of history.

Samuel's life demonstrates God's willingness to allow us go through seasons of chaos and confusion to help us become sensitive enough to hear God's call so we can have order and clarity in our lives. When the path of our lives makes sense, flowing mostly according to our designs, we rarely spend much time deeply discerning God's call. On the other hand, when we walk through seasons of darkness, confusion, and disillusionment, we suddenly find ourselves searching and groping for the light of God's call, which alone can bring true meaning and purpose to our lives.

Out of Confusion, Clarity

I am no stranger to the experience of finding clarity only after seasons of confusion. When I left home for college, I was riding on a spiritual high. During my final years in high school, my faith had been transformed from a basic system of beliefs and ethical standards to a living relationship with a gracious, loving God. I was surrounded by a great youth group at my local church and by Christian friends at school who cared about having fun and being faithful to God. Now I was headed to a religious college where I was expecting the same supportive fellowship and intimate experiences of God's presence. Life was good.

When I arrived on campus, I met other wonderfully faithful Christian students and found a church with a strong campus ministry. Still, something was missing. For some time, God had felt close to me and I had been able to clearly see God guiding my life. I now found myself in a situation where I was questioning who I was, who I should be hanging out with, what principles I should base my life upon, and what career path to follow. As I wrestled with these big questions, God appeared to be disturbingly silent no matter how hard I pressed my head into my hands as I prayed.

My plan for some time was to be an engineer, but my science and math classes just were not doing it for me. I was accustomed to having strong core groups of friends to rely on. Now I was hanging out with several different friend groups unsure of which group I fit into or if I fit into any group at all. I was raised in a household where my family ate dinner together every night and by parents whose advice I could rely on — though I generally pretended to resent it — a sharp contrast to my present reality of eating each meal with a different group of students, none of whom seemed to know much more than I did about navigating college life.

My prayer life changed too. A few months earlier, I had been so enthralled with God's goodness that I would be excited to wake up and pray in the mornings. It had not been uncommon for me to find myself overcome with feelings of acceptance, protection, and love as I read the scripture and prayed. All that changed overnight. I still prayed each day, though it suddenly seemed like nothing more than a mindless chore. I found myself wondering if my prayers went anywhere beyond the cold cinder block walls of my dorm room.

I could not clearly see or feel God. I was 250 miles from home at a college where I did not really know anyone. I was lost.

Something strange happened as I persevered in prayer during that difficult first semester away from home; God spoke. Only this time, God did not speak through warm sensations of acceptance or a dramatic vision of what my life could be. I received no audible words from God, and strong feelings of assurance were absent from my spiritual life at the time. Still, God spoke.

God initially spoke through silence and a sense of His absence as I learned what it meant to follow a God that I could not see, feel, or touch. Several months into this journey of listening to God's silence and seeking a seemingly absent deity, I began to think that maybe God was calling me to vocational ministry.

At this point, I was quite insecure in my sense of calling because I figured that people who were called to ministry must be better at hearing God speak than I seemed to be at the time. I assumed that anyone legitimately called to pastoral ministry should have a better sense of their own identity and a more intimate connection to God than I possessed at the time. Thankfully, though I tried a thousand times to disqualify myself from ministry, I could not shake the thought that perhaps it was the career path I was supposed to pursue.

So, I took the only step forward that I could find — to schedule a visit with my college chaplain. I felt silly walking into his office. I wondered if all my ideas about ministry were simply a subconscious reaction to my anxiety about the need to hurry up and pick a major. I replayed in my mind how it would feel if after I shared my thoughts, my chaplain tells me that I must have heard God wrong because he was not sure I was cut out for such work.

Imagine my surprise after I nervously rambled through my articulation of a sense of calling when my chaplain smiled through his oversized mustache and said, "Wil, you'll be a great one."

At this moment, the clouds of doubt and distance disappeared. As my chaplain spoke, I clearly heard the Holy Spirit saying, "You have heard the call correctly. Now, go prepare yourself for it." From that moment, God began to feel real, close, and present once again.

Looking back on it, I am thankful that God forced me to look for Him through his absence and listen to Him in His silence during this formative season in my life. In so doing, God gave me a gift that I could not have received otherwise. Now when I go through seasons when my spirit feels dry, I remember that sometimes when it feels like God is absent, He is powerfully present doing some of His most important work.

Out of Defiance, Reliance

For Samuel and for us hearing God's voice clearly once does not mean that we will always be able to understand His ways in the future. Decades after first hearing God's call as a young boy in the darkness of a corrupted temple, Samuel found himself again struggling to find God's way forward for the people of Israel.

Having served for decades as Israel's most powerful judge and prophet, Samuel made plans to relinquish his position and allow his sons to govern. However, the people of Israel had other ideas. They no longer wanted judges and prophets. They wanted a king like the other nations had.

Few propositions could have been as hurtful to Samuel as this one. The whole purpose of the people of Israel was to be a people set aside to make known the identity of the one true God. They were not supposed to follow the ways of man, but the ways of God. Their only king was God. By appointing a man to be king, they would become like the other nations and forfeit much of what made them unique, special, and chosen.

In exasperation, Samuel turned to God in prayer. God graciously spoke to Samuel, informing him that the demand for a king was indeed a rejection of God's design for Israel. However, God was powerful enough to use even Israel's acts of defiance to increase their reliance on Him. Through the blessings and the curses of earthly kings, God would show the people the very nature of their heavenly king. So, God instructed Samuel to anoint Saul to be king over Israel (1 Samuel 8-10).

Like Samuel, we sometimes encounter situations where it is hard to see how God can have His way in the world.

Out of Shambles, Surrender

With her life in the balance, Logan had finally quit running from God. Years of addiction and despair had taken their toll on her health and her ability to maintain custody of the child she adored. So, she took one of the few options left to her and began going to the 12-step meetings at the nearby church. Eventually, after a few starts and stops, she found God blessing her with a life of sobriety and joy she never knew existed.

Now, here she was again, pulled over on the side of the road with blue lights flashing behind her. She was doing almost everything right. She was attending recovery meetings; she was going to church; she was praying every day; she was putting her child's needs ahead of her own; she was hanging out around positive influences; and she was continuing her education so she could support herself. Everyone who knew her saw a new person; a hope-filled, peaceful, beautiful person.

How could this happen now? She had taken a small short-cut and it caught up with her massively. Driving with a suspended license was not an easily resolvable matter for someone with her prior record. As the police officer approached the car, she turned off the Vacation Bible School soundtrack she and her son had been enjoying and prepared herself to fight once more for her life and livelihood.

When all the legal ramifications of her past were said and done, Logan was forced to plead guilty to a felony DUI. Resolving the charge would require jail time away from her son, jeopardize her ability to further her education, limit her future employment options, and shake the foundation of her fledgling faith.

It was hard for Logan to understand how everything she loved and valued could be taken away from her when she was finally doing everything possible to live right. Jail is not an easy place for anyone and it was especially hard for Logan. After spending the last year distancing herself from negative influences, she found herself surrounded once more by negativity, and her refusal to engage in negative talk made finding friends almost impossible. Knowing the love of real friends and a real church family waiting for her on the outside made the isolation of being inside that much harder. Logan was angry, resentful, and confused. Even so, she was not ready to give up.

Through prayer and conversations with her pastor, Logan began to see that God would not always remove her struggles, but God would always see her through these struggles. In those difficult days, she made a commitment to surrender herself completely to God's will; no more turning back, no more looking for shortcuts, no more trying to find an easy way out.

Not only did Logan's total surrender to God allow her to maintain her sanity and sobriety, it enabled her to feel the burning desire God had placed in her heart to help others who had become so crippled by addiction that their lives could only be saved by wholeheartedly surrendering to God. Upon her release, she set out with single-minded dedication to the task God had given her.

Today, Logan lives in a beautiful log cabin where she and her husband lovingly raise their family of four. She is a highly-respected member of her church and community. Whenever she goes to work each day, she helps others leave their nightmares behind and awaken to God's dreams for them.

Out of Despair, Hope

For some time after Samuel anointed Saul king of Israel, life seemed to be proceeding along a logical path. King Saul was leading the people of Israel into becoming more politically powerful, which in turn was spreading their religious influence. Samuel could look back and see how God was working, through this new king, in a way he could never have anticipated.

However, the people of Israel would have to deal with the curses as well as the blessings of having an earthly king. In Saul's case, the blessings came first and the curses came after. Over the years, power and greed corrupted Saul's heart. He became more concerned with his own wealth than the well-being of the people. Worse yet, he began to disregard the ways of God.

As you might imagine, Samuel was disconsolate. After having his entire world-view torn apart by the people's demand for a king, Saul was the king God had led Samuel to anoint. Saul was the one God was supposed to work through to establish a righteous kingdom, to save the people from their own unfaithful designs, and to preserve Israel's mission to make known the one true God. Now, Saul had failed and

Samuel could not see a way for God to redeem Israel from their mess.

Then one day, in the midst of Samuel's despair, God confronts him saying: "How long will you mourn for Saul, since I have rejected him as king over Israel? Fill your horn with oil and be on your way; I am sending you to Jesse of Bethlehem. I have chosen one of his sons to be king (1 Samuel 16:1)." Apparently, God was not sitting in heaven overwrought with anxiety and confusion because a human king turned away from the path of faithfulness. Unlike Samuel, God knew people well enough to be aware of the possibility of even the best people failing, and God loved people enough to offer another chance for them to turn back to Him. It was time for Samuel to move past his grief and self-pity over the failures of Saul and get on with the business of helping God's newly anointed leader, David, come to power.

Out of Endings, Beginnings

If we live long enough, we will all go through times like Samuel; times when we see no way for God's will to be carried out in our lives. This was certainly the case for Elizabeth.

Elizabeth and Bob Gillespie had a romance no Hollywood script could match. Raised during the Great Depression, Elizabeth knew that Bob did not have the means to buy her a diamond ring for their engagement, so she saved her own money and went to town to purchase a tiny diamond ring for him to give her. That very day as they rode the bus back home from the town where they had been shopping, Elizabeth realized that Bob had also secretly purchased a ring which cost him the equivalent of several months of savings. Not wanting to hurt her soon to be fiancé's feelings with the realization

13

that she had doubted his ability to provide a ring, Elizabeth discreetly stuffed the ring she had bought in the crease of the bus seat and left it there. Even when finances were as tight as could be, she placed bolstering her husband's confidence above boosting her bank account.

Bob soon became a Methodist pastor, and together he and Elizabeth faithfully served in 19 different charges while moving in and out of 17 different parsonages over 41 years of faithful ministry. At home, Elizabeth would sweep clean the dirt floors, and more than once, she found herself praying that a church member would drop off a side of beef or vegetables from the garden because they lacked the money to purchase their groceries at the store. At church, Elizabeth would organize the congregations and outlying communities to offer the children Vacation Bible School, a new ministry program at the time which was sweeping the nation.

In days of difficulty and days of ease, Bob and Elizabeth found their love for God, for each other, and for their precious daughter, Margaret, to be more than enough to see them through. Elizabeth was in her early 80s on the dreadful day she stood over Bob's grave to say goodbye. She thanked God for all the good years they had together and she went home convinced that her life was over.

With Bob gone, Elizabeth prepared for her health to give out and for the Lord to call her home. She simply could not see any future for herself in a life without Bob.

While Elizabeth waited to die, days turned into weeks, weeks turned into months, and her health remained strong. Finally, she decided that if God was not going to take her life, He must have something left for her to accomplish. Elizabeth was not sure what difference a single elderly woman could make, but she decided to find out.

After seeking God's guidance in prayer, Elizabeth felt led to reach out to the many young girls in her local church. One thing led to another, and soon there were a bunch of excitable rambunctious little girls running around her apartment several times a year for "Granny G's Teas." While the girls enjoyed being served tea, with plenty of sugar, and fancy snacks on Elizabeth's finest china, Elizabeth used the opportunity to tell Bible stories and share how God's promises had been proven true to her throughout her life.

A few years ago, Elizabeth's church invited the community to join them in celebrating her one-hundredth birthday. By this time, the young girls who once learned the finer point of serving tea from Elizabeth had grown into beautiful, confident young women preparing to graduate high school and pursue their dreams. One by one, they came through the line to embrace Elizabeth and to share how her tea parties helped them to find a foundation of faith that they were trusting to guide them through the new chapters in their lives.

When it looked as if Elizabeth's life was ending, God was only just beginning to do one of His most powerful works through her.

Out of Darkness, Light

Samuel first heard God's call in the darkness of night. Centuries later, wise men followed a light in the darkness to lead them to Bethlehem to worship a child whose life provided the world with a light that the darkness can never extinguish. Still today, God speaks to people like us who are caught in the darkness of confusion and despair.

When I go outside at night, I am reminded that without

15

the darkness, the stars would not be visible, and without their light, we would never be able to chart our place in the universe. Could it be that God uses seasons of darkness to help us to clearly see our place in His kingdom?

Reflection Questions

What seasons of darkness have you been through?

How have you learned to listen for God during those seasons of darkness?

When have your plans for life been derailed?

How has God blessed you even after your best plans failed?

CHAPTER TWO

Amos: Man of the Cloth

by Kevin Slimp

[22] Even though you bring me burnt offerings and grain offerings, I will not accept them. Though you bring choice fellowship offerings, I will have no regard for them. [23] Away with the noise of your songs! I will not listen to the music of your harps.
[24] But let justice roll on like a river, righteousness like a never-failing stream!

Amos 5:22-24 (NIV)

Primer

Have you ever attended a rally or protest where someone was speaking out against some type of injustice?

Have you ever encountered a situation that made you speak out concerning an injustice?

What type of injustices are prevalent in the world today?

Man of the Cloth? Not in his own eyes.

Those of you reading this chapter with more than five decades under your belts probably remember a song by Jerry Reed titled, "Amos Moses." This song tells the story of a one-armed Cajun alligator hunter named Amos Moses, who was "named after a man of the cloth."

If you were like me as a youngster listening to that song,

you probably assumed Reed was referring to Moses as the man of the cloth, and you would be partially correct. But Reed obviously knew his Old Testament better than most.

Even though Amos would have never described himself as a man of the cloth, this book of the Old Testament stands out as the story of a simple man pulled away from his comfortable life to answer God's call, even though it probably wasn't his first choice.

The Book of Amos is the earliest of the twelve books commonly referred to as "the minor prophets," but a quick reading of the nine chapters making up this book should convince any reader that Amos is anything but "minor." Disappearing from the Biblical story almost as soon as he appeared, his saga takes place around 750 BCE during the reign of Jeroboam II, making Amos the first biblical prophetic book written.

So, what was it that caused Dr. Martin Luther King, Jr. to be moved so much by Amos Chapter 5 that he quoted Amos during his "I have a dream" speech?

A Simple Man, Not a professional prophet.

We learn in Amos 1:1 that Amos was from Tekoa, a small village in Judah not far from Bethlehem and Jerusalem. He wasn't a member of the priestly elite like Ezekiel or Jeremiah, nor did he serve in the court like Isaiah.

Amos, it seems, earned his living from working with the flock and in the fruit grove. Whether he worked as a hired hand or owned his own land, is unknown. We learn in Amos 7 that he was working with his flock when God took him away.

Amos himself tells us he didn't seek to be a prophet and had no intention of spending his time chastising the people in the name of God. But someone had different ideas, and that's just what Amos found himself doing.

Though his home was in Judah, we learn he was "sent" to announce God's judgment on Israel, the northern kingdom. Though he was speaking to a particular audience, his words are addressed to all of Israel.

And what did God have to say that caused Amos to leave his home and work to travel north? Amos wastes no time in getting right to the point:

> [3] This is what the Lord says: "For three sins of Damascus, even for four, I will not relent.
> Because she threshed Gilead with sledges having iron teeth,
> [4] I will send fire on the house of Hazael that will consume the fortresses of Ben-Hadad.
> [5] I will break down the gate of Damascus; I will destroy the king who is in the Valley of Aven, and the one who holds the scepter in Beth Eden. The people of Aram will go into exile to Kir," says the Lord.
>
> Amos 1:3-5 (NIV)

Instead of backing off, Amos seems to pick up steam as he moves from Chapter 1 to Chapter 2. It seems as if no one is going to get off easy as Amos continues to declare God's judgment on Israel:

> [13] "Now then, I will crush you as a cart crushes when loaded with grain.
> [14] The swift will not escape, the strong will not muster their strength, and the warrior will not save his life.
> [15] The archer will not stand his ground, the fleet-footed soldier will not get away, and the horseman will not save his life.
> [16] Even the bravest warriors will flee naked on that day," declares the Lord.
>
> Amos 2:13-15 (NIV)

Amos wasn't about to win a popularity contest with judgments like those. His skill with words and the broad range of his general knowledge of history and the world let us know that Amos is no ignorant peasant.

I fell in love with the Book of Amos as a college student. During an Old Testament class, I was required to write a research paper about a minor prophet. I basically flipped a coin and selected Amos. As I studied his book and researched background material, I began to gain a sense of this shepherd and sycamore farmer's life.

I imagined when his produce was ready for market, he traveled to various villages in nearby Israel. In the more rural areas, he would observe the hardships imposed on the working class by the wealthy landowners who lived in comparative luxury in the larger cities. When his travels took him into the larger cities, Amos was deeply troubled by the disparities between the rich and the poor. Even more disturbing, it seems, Amos was outraged when he observed the ways religious and political leaders attempted to justify this disparity.

It seems that Amos was a lot like me. I often dream at night about things that bothered me during the previous day. Problems at work, home, and issues with those I encounter often lead to sleepless nights. Nearly every morning I wake to a vivid dream. Sometimes they are troubling. I imagine Amos must have often roused to disturbing dreams.

In the book bearing his name, three of his dreams and visions are recorded. In the first, Amos sees a man with a plumb line measuring a wall that is about to topple. Soon, the man is told the bulging wall is the house of Israel. Amos realized this dream wasn't about a wall. It was about the nation of Israel. As surely as the wall was about to tumble, so Israel would soon fall into captivity.

In a second vision, Israel is represented by a basket of summer fruit that represents the people, who are living a prosperous life represented by the ripe fruit. But we all know what happens to ripe fruit eventually. If not eaten, it rots and decays in time. Amos preached that the peaceful years of the Israelite nation were coming to an end.

In his third vision, in which a swarm of locusts were about to devour all of the land's produce, Israel was being warned about the evil days that lay ahead.

Amos could keep his dreams and visions secret for only so long. By Chapter 5, it seems Amos has no choice but to declare God's judgment on his listeners:

> [21] "I hate, I despise your religious festivals; your assemblies are a stench to me.
> [22] Even though you bring me burnt offerings and grain offerings, I will not accept them.
> Though you bring choice fellowship offerings, I will have no regard for them.
> [23] Away with the noise of your songs! I will not listen to the music of your harps.
> [24] But let justice roll on like a river, righteousness like a never-failing stream!
>
> Amos 5:21-24 (NIV)

You can read all of Amos for yourself and see that he wasn't enjoying the message he was compelled to deliver. He had a much greater reason for sharing his words with the people of Israel.

Amos, you see, was a true prophet. He was a spokesperson for God. It becomes increasingly clear that Amos had no desire to entertain or please his listeners. He spoke for one simple reason... God was calling him to speak.

The priests of his time would be no fans of Amos. As he spoke concerning their solemn assemblies, public prayers, and sacrifices, it's clear that Amos was making more enemies than friends as he spoke to his audience of strangers.

Here is the reason I fell in love with Amos as I wrote that research paper so many years go: Amos was authentic. He had no desire to leave his homeland and address the people of the northern kingdom. I'm quite certain he would have much rather been home, watching his sheep or tending his garden.

However, seeing the injustices taking place around him obviously made Amos uncomfortable. Witnessing the hypocrisy of the religious and political leaders was more than he could stand. At some point, directed by God, Amos got up, made the journey to Israel, and addressed the crowds.

Was he popular? Probably not. Maybe by some, but certainly not by the elite of the day. More than likely, many looked at him as a mad person.

The words of Amos sting. Not just to Israel. I'm convinced, as was Dr. Martin Luther King, Jr., that the words of Amos are as true today as they were thousands of years ago. Social injustice, so prevalent in our world, continues to this day. Religious and political leaders still make excuses for tolerating injustice.

We don't hear about Amos again after his experience in these nine chapters. I always imagined he said his peace, packed his bag, and went home. That's what I like about Amos. He heard God's call through the suffering around him. He answered God's call, then disappeared from the scene.

Chapter 9 ends with a word of hope. Eventually, Israel will be destroyed, but not before great suffering takes place. The captives will return home. The cities will be rebuilt. Gardens and fruit will return.

I like to think that Amos' story didn't end at verse 15 of Chapter 9. My guess is that he continued to dream and have visions. How he reacted to those dreams, we don't know. Not yet.

A minor prophet? Perhaps. But only because the pages that make up the book of Amos are few. In my thinking, Amos stands tall with all of the prophets who left their comfortable homes to speak out for God.

Reflection Questions

Have you ever been so upset about an unjust event or situation that it caused you to have dreams about it?

How would you compare Amos to other prophets of the Old Testament? What strikes you as different about him?

What are the injustices in your community or society at large that you feel compelled to address?

CHAPTER THREE

Rahab: Fulfilling Her Call

by Rev. Dr. Aleze M. Fulbright

²⁵ But Joshua spared Rahab the prostitute, with her family and all who belonged to her, because she hid the men Joshua had sent as spies to Jericho—and she lives among the Israelites to this day.

Joshua 6:25 (NIV)

Suggested Readings: Joshua 2:1-24; Joshua 6:20-25;

Matthew 1:5; Hebrews 11:31; James 2:25-26

Primer

What is an example of a time when you lived out your faith in action?

Is there something in your past that seems to keep you from living out your faith?

Understanding Call

One of the familiar quotes regarding call comes to mind, "One's call should not be mistaken for one's job. A call is bigger than what we do for a living. It defines God's intentions for our lives."

As a small child, I was often told that God could only use those who were perfect; those who lived a perfect life and did nothing wrong in the eyes of God and humanity. As I was introduced to the faithful giants of the Bible and even some of my (s)heroes of real life, it seemed that these persons had it all together. As I saw them, their lives were in order, as they possessed outrageous courage and an unwavering faith to follow God. So often, I would equate these personas as the litmus for how God can call, much less use, anyone for God's service and witness. It is when I took a reflective look at the biblical character of Rahab that my perspective changed about who God calls and how God can use all persons for God's greater purposes.

Understanding Rahab

To be uncommon, one knows they are out of the ordinary, unusual and rare. Being uncommon means: looking at the same things everyone else sees and thinking something different, testing common assumptions, nurturing relentless curiosity, continually exiting comfort zones, and creating opportunities, not waiting for them to happen. It is evident from the text an uncommon encounter by uncommon people yielded uncommon success.

"Joshua, Nun's son, secretly sent two men as spies from Shittim. He said, "Go. Look over the land, especially Jericho." They set out and entered the house of a prostitute named Rahab. They bedded down there" (Joshua 2:1 CEB). Who is this Canaanite woman who collaborated with the people of God, at a critical time, to not only save them, but also save herself and her family?

Rahab was a business owner, who many suggest, had a house built in the high wall around Jericho, which was used as a place of rest for weary travelers entering the city. Other scholars suggest that Rahab may have been a temple prostitute, which in Canaanite eyes was an acceptable line of work. It is also suggested that prostitution was the last resort for desperate women, who had few ways to support themselves if they did not marry. Perhaps, Rahab's career choice, as an innkeeper or a harlot, came from her need to survive and support herself and her family.

Understanding Rahab's Call

Rahab would be the most uncommon character for God to call for service to and in service with God's people. Despite being female, a foreigner, and her claim to fame, Rahab was an independent business woman, whose faith is manifested not only in words, but also in actions. Rahab's call is demonstrated by 3Rs--- Risk –Taking Mission and Service ("But the woman had taken the two men and hidden them. Then she said, "Of course the men came to me. But I didn't know where they were from"-Joshua 2:4); Radical Hospitality ("But she had taken them up to the roof and hidden them under the flax stalks that she had laid out on the roof"-Joshua 2:6); along with Relentless Faith in God ("I know that the Lord has given you the land. Terror over you has overwhelmed us. The entire population of the land has melted down in fear because of you. We have heard how the Lord dried up the water of the Reed Sea in front of you when you left Egypt. We have also heard what you did to Sihon and Og, the two kings of the Amorites on the other side of the Jordan. You utterly wiped them out. We heard this and our hearts turned to water. Because of you, people can no longer work up their courage. This is because the Lord your God is God in heaven above and on earth below"- Joshua 2:9-11).

Rahab's faith, courage, and concern for others saved her family and herself. Transformed by God's call, Rahab experienced conversion from harlot to heroine, and Rahab is an inspiration. Rahab was brave, decisive, and quick to give orders. In addition, there are scriptural references that call Rahab worthy, listing her by name in the hallmark of faith (Hebrews 11:31). Because of Rahab's faith, God saved her in every sense of the word. Rahab gave birth to a son, Boaz, who married a woman named Ruth, the great-grandmother of King David. Ultimately, Rahab is listed in the first chapter of Matthew's Gospel in the lineage of Jesus.

"Maybe the name prostitute does not matter so much to God. The authors emphasized her sinfulness, but perhaps God saw a woman who did what she had to do to save herself and her family. God saw the courageous choices she made to help the spies. In God's vocabulary, maybe her name was not Rahab the prostitute, but Rahab the faithful, Rahab the courageous, Rahab the quick-thinking negotiator, or Rahab the wise" (Preaching the Women of the Old Testament, p.68).

Understanding Our Response

The call is often equated to that of pulpit ministry or becoming a missionary overseas, when in fact, the varying expressions of God's call can be lived out by God's grace through everyday means of service, and by varying types of people. The celebration to the call of uncommon people is the willing response to utilize our God-given gifts and graces, skills and abilities, and resources to manifest the Gospel Message.

As quoted above, "One's call should not be mistaken for one's job. A call is bigger than what we do for a living. It defines God's intentions for our lives." When reading about this faithful woman, she is often referred as "Rahab the prostitute," but the negative label and the actions of her past did not determine her destiny. Rahab's example demonstrates a living faith in a forgiving and grace-filled God. Without a doubt, Rahab helped to save the lives of the Israelite spies, which in turn set Israel on the path toward the Promise Land. May we not be so quick to determine who God can use for God's greater purposes. May we not confine God and who God calls to our societal boxes, which contain our comforts and certain characteristics. May we see the potential in all people, and how God can mend the broken pieces of our lives, to be an uncommon witness of God's great care and unconditional love.

Reflection Questions

Rahab risked everything to live into and out of her calling. What risks are you willing to take for the sake of God's calling?

Responding to God's call requires faith, as evident through the witness of Rahab. At what point do we allow our faith to overtake our fears as we respond to God's call?

How do we often identify or alienate a person's call potential simply by her or his past behaviors or activities?

Bibliography

- Japinga, Lynn. Preaching the Women of the Old Testament: Who They Were and Why They Matter. First Edition. ed. Louisville, Kentucky: Westminster John Knox Press, 2017.
- Nowell, Irene. Women in the Old Testament. Collegeville, Minn.: Liturgical Press, 1997.
- Taylor, Marion Ann, and Christiana De Groot, eds. Women of War, Women of Woe : Joshua and Judges through the Eyes of Nineteenth-Century Female Biblical Interpreters. Grand Rapids, Michigan: William Eerdmans Publishing Company, 2016.

CHAPTER FOUR

David: A Man After God's Own Heart

by Rob Couch

³² David said to Saul, "Let no one lose heart on account of this Philistine; your servant will go and fight him."

³³ Saul replied, "You are not able to go out against this Philistine and fight him; you are only a young man, and he has been a warrior from his youth."

³⁴ But David said to Saul, "Your servant has been keeping his father's sheep. When a lion or a bear came and carried off a sheep from the flock, ³⁵ I went after it, struck it and rescued the sheep from its mouth. When it turned on me, I seized it by its hair, struck it and killed it. ³⁶ Your servant has killed both the lion and the bear; this uncircumcised Philistine will be like one of them, because he has defied the armies of the living God. ³⁷ The Lord who rescued me from the paw of the lion and the paw of the bear will rescue me from the hand of this Philistine."

Saul said to David, "Go, and the Lord be with you."

1 Samuel 17:32-37 (NIV)

> ## Primer
>
> **Who is your favorite Biblical figure?**
>
> **Were they called to do something by God?**
>
> **What about your favorite Biblical figure reminds you of your own story?**

Call me son!

"You may just have the call, son." These were the words spoken to me by a faithful church member immediately after I gave one of my first sermons at the youth group led Easter Sunrise service. As a sixteen-year-old, standing in the amphitheater of our local college campus, it was a lot to take in. I had always loved doing things at the church. I enjoyed opportunities for leading and speaking, but this was the moment I began to wonder if God was calling me to full-time Christian ministry. To be honest, I really didn't know what "the call" was, but over the course of the next several years, I began to hear more clearly that God was calling me to enter the ministry.

This is often how God's call comes to our lives, from the

mouths of other people. Over years of ministry, I've known a handful who've told me that they've heard God call them to do something in a very direct, even audible way. Most of the time, in my experience, God speaks to us through the people around us. For some of us, it might be hard to hear God's call any other way. Often we don't feel worthy enough or bold enough to embark on such a journey. Sometimes, even our friends and family, those who know us best, have a hard time imagining God would call us. I remember after telling my mom and dad that I wanted to enter the ministry, they spent a decent amount of time trying to talk me out of it. They would say, "Are you sure you want to do this?" and "Do you know how challenging ministry can be?" Interestingly, God used a man I barely knew to speak God's call into my life first.

David's struggles

I've always loved the stories of King David's life. Though most of us have never been a king or warrior, David's well-known struggles with coveting, failing God, covering things up, and strained relationships with family members are pretty familiar to most of us. I think many of us find it refreshing to know that a person with so much baggage can also be someone the Bible describes as a "man after God's own heart." If this is true for David, then it can be true for us as well. Despite our foibles and failings, God's grace can still redeem and call our hearts.

God's great surprise

One of my favorite David stories has to do with his

selection as God's next anointed king. The Bible is full of great surprises, and the choosing of David was one of the best surprises of all. God rejected King Saul as King, so God told Samuel to go and anoint the new king of Israel among Jesse's sons in Bethlehem. I can picture the scene as Jesse's sons proudly line up to be inspected by Samuel and possibly chosen: heads held high, chests puffed out. I imagine it to be reminiscent of that familiar childhood experience of picking teams. Everyone is anxious to be selected, and no one would want to be picked last. One by one Jesse's sons pass by Samuel. Eliab starts it off. He must have been the most impressive of Jesse's sons because when he walks by Samuel says, "Surely the LORD's anointed is now before the LORD" (1 Samuel 16:6). God's response to Samuel's assumptions was profound, "Do not look on his appearance or on the height of his stature, because I have rejected him; for the LORD does not see as mortals see; they look on the outward appearance, but the LORD looks on the heart" (1 Samuel 16:7). One by one the sons pass by Samuel for inspection. Seven sons pass by, and none of them are to be God's anointed. Samuel asks the obvious question to Jesse, "Are these all the sons you have?" There was one more. Seemingly too young, small and unimportant to even make it into the lineup, the one tasked with shepherding the sheep was definitely not King material. They send for Jesse's youngest son, David, and he passes before Samuel. Surprise, David is the Lord's anointed.

We are often surprised by God when people are called into ministry. I imagine that Jesse and his seven other sons were flabbergasted and a little embarrassed that they hadn't seen it. I'm sure it was surprising enough that God wanted another King anointed while Saul was still in power. Of all the people in Bethlehem, of all the people in Israel and Judah, David would have been among the most unlikely of choices.

God often calls the unlikely to do the extraordinary. I've seen this again and again throughout my years of ministry. I've seen God call a retired military couple who imagined that most of their golden years would be spent RVing around the country to start a new ministry to feed hungry children in their community. I've seen God call a mom and dad who had a family member ravaged by addiction to start a substance abuse recovery program for their community that has helped hundreds of people turn to Christ and find hope in the midst of devastating circumstances. Again and again, I've seen God call the unlikely to do the extraordinary. Most people, including those who answered God's call, would not have guessed that they were the ones that God was anointing to do such important work.

Looking inward instead of outward

One of the primary reasons we don't recognize God's call in our own lives or in the lives of others is that we, like Samuel, are obsessed with the outward appearance. I find it interesting that this preoccupation with outward appearances has spanned thousands of years. In a world today that can be obsessed with choosing the right Facebook profile picture and achieving the perfect angle for our next selfie, our preoccupation with outward appearances has taken on epidemic status. Most of us have an idea in our mind of what a person called by God looks like. Perhaps it's a person of a certain age, gender, attractiveness, or ability. Maybe we think God only calls those who have it all together. Sometimes, it seems, the person we feel is least likely called by God is the one staring at us in the mirror. God says to us as he said to Samuel long ago, "The LORD does not see as mortals see; they look on the outward appearance, but the LORD looks on the heart."

David wasn't without great qualities. In fact, when he arrives on the scene, and Samuel lays his eyes on him, the initial reports were good, in spite of David's age. We're told that David "was ruddy, and had beautiful eyes, and was handsome" (1 Samuel 16:12). In addition to these outwardly apparent qualities we learn throughout David's life that he could develop great friendships, was brave, a great leader, and could admit (in time) that he was wrong. In fact, had Samuel arrived on the scene a few years later, perhaps David would have been in the front of the line. Again, however, we have to be careful with outward appearances and look at the heart of the person. In fact, I think sometimes we miss God's calling in ourselves and others not because we don't look the part, but because the world sees us as destined for some other sort of "greatness." Over my years of ministry, I've met many doctors, lawyers, and business people who were blessed with so many qualities that their teachers, their families, and their friends assumed they were destined for material wealth and societal success. Years later, I would meet these kinds of people in seminary, pursuing vocational ministry as a second career and hear them tell stories of how they once heard God's calling, but that the siren call of another kind of success drowned it out.

Blinded by success

Success can blind us from answering God's call. Success often begets success, and along with it come long hours, deep sacrifices, and complicated lives. Pastors are sometimes guilty of being blinded by the success of their people and then not recognizing God's call in them. We may have low expectations of our busiest, most successful people thinking they are too

busy for God's call. However, there are few things more exhila-
rating than seeing a wildly successful person pivot their lives
and focus their talents and energy in the direction that God
is calling them. Years ago, a member of our church answered
God's call to be part of a medical mission team to Costa Rica.
He had a successful surgical practice in our town, but when
he returned from the trip, he kept asking, "Why can't we do
the same sort of ministry for the people who live here in our
own community?" As he awakened to the plight of the thousands of uninsured people in our city who could not go to a
doctor, he heard God's call to start a medical clinic that would
provide top quality healthcare for the uninsured. He left his
practice to direct this clinic which still operates today. Thousands and thousands of people have received medical care and
experienced the love of Christ as they were cared for in his
clinic. This surgeon has a whole new understanding of success.

Fighting giants in your own life

Another chapter of David's story also describes, in a more
heroic way, God's call on his life. The familiar story of David
and Goliath further illustrates the unlikely calling of David as
God's anointed. Foolishly, David volunteers to face the Philistine's gigantic champion. After a period of significant doubt,
and coming to a point of desperation, Saul agrees to put a
small boy on the battlefield and places the battle and the future
of his kingdom in his hands. Initially, the Israelites want
David to fight the way Saul fights with heavy armor and a
massive sword, but in the end, David answers God's call in the
way which fits him best. With great courage, he took the tools
of his trade onto the battlefield and knocked down the giant.

As you reflect on God's call on your life, don't forget to

look for the giants others are unwilling to face. Many of our churches and communities are faced with seemingly impossible problems that people are afraid or unwilling to do anything about. Seek God's help in finding the courage to go to the front lines and face them, even if no one else will. Don't be surprised, however, if people resist your efforts. David's older brother, Eliab, wished for David to mind his own business and go back to his place tending the sheep. Many a person trying to answer God's call in the church have been shut down by pastors or other church leaders for both benevolent and malevolent reasons. And, when these gatekeepers do permit us to follow God's lead, they often demand that we do it their way under the weight of a million dos and don'ts which slow us down or prevent us from moving forward successfully.

Free prayers

I'll never forget one of my greatest regrets in ministry. One of our members came to me with an unusual idea. He wanted to sit by the road in front of our church with a sign that reads, "Free Prayer," then wait and pray with anyone who pulled over for the offer. As I listened to his peculiar idea, I quickly began strategizing how to direct his desire to pray for others into a more conventional ministry.

I could just imagine the strange looks of those driving by and the great disappointment he would face when no one stopped, or worse, when people shouted insults at him from open car windows. I quickly devised a plan that would be sure to stop him. I suggested that we take his idea to a committee. I knew it would work; committees are deadly accurate at killing creativity and innovation. It worked perfectly. I can remember even congratulating myself on how well I handled that bizarre request. After a few years of reflection and maturity, however, I realized I had made a terrible mistake. I've wondered ever since what might have happened if my faith-filled member had been encouraged to follow God's call. A popular business leadership book by Michael Masterson is entitled *Ready, Fire, Aim.* When answering God's call, sometimes, this may be the best order to follow. Waiting for all the right permissions and all the perfect conditions may mean never getting to fire at all!

God looks inside

David's story reminds us that God's call can come to any and all of us because God doesn't look on the outside like most of our world does, instead, God looks on the heart. Many of us miss God's call because when we look in the mirror, we aren't able to see all that God sees. Others miss hearing God's call because the world around us has predetermined what success looks like for us, and their vision of success falls so short of what God can see. We, even pastors and church leaders, cannot see how God is calling others because our vision becomes so marred with things that don't ultimately matter. God's call courageously beckons us to the front lines to face the giants others are unwilling to face. When we answer this call, we say with David, "You come to me with sword and spear and javelin; but I come to you in the name of the Lord of hosts…this day the Lord will deliver you into my hand…" Ignoring the naysayers and with the tools we know best, we stand up to face the giants while answering God's call on our lives.

Reflection Questions

What are some giants that need slaying in your life?

David was anything but perfect. Yet he found a way to become a man after God's own heart. What are some things you can do to become closer to God?

What is God calling you to do right now?

CHAPTER FIVE

Joseph: An Interpreter of Dreams

by Larry Ousley

"The story of Joseph is the most beautiful story in all the world."

Leo Tolstoy

Primer

Have you ever had a dream that seemed so real it seemed to follow you through your day?

How would you feel if you woke up from your dreams one morning to realize that you were now a slave in a foreign land?

Let's go on an inner journey. For a moment, imagine you are in prison. That's where Joseph found himself.

Although your life had such great promise even from childhood, you also feel the pain of having been rejected all your life by parts of your family. Your brothers made fun of you, ganged up on you, and eventually even sold you into slavery.

After being sold into slavery, you were assigned to a wealthy household as a servant only to have the wife of the wealthy person try to make love to you, and when you resisted, she accused you of trying to rape her, and you were thrown into prison.

How would you feel? What would you do? Would you feel your life was over and that God had abandoned you in your time of need?

44

Joseph's responses to these overwhelming setbacks serve as inspirations to us and clues as to how you make meaning of life events, how you discern God's call for your life, and how you live it out.

Joseph's story occupies the largest portion of Genesis of any of the narratives of the great fathers and mothers of the Hebrew tradition. The last fourteen chapters of Genesis (chapters 37-50) give the accounts of Joseph's heroic life. In addition to its being the longest narrative primarily about one person, it is the only portion of Genesis written by a single author. At least this is true of chapters 37-45 with a few later additions in chapters 46-50. The first 36 chapters of Genesis are interwoven from ancient sources from 1000 to 400 BCE. For example, two creation stories exist in the Bible with similarities and differences. The first comes from the P source and the second from the J source.

Also, Joseph may well be the oldest of all the sources being written sometime between 1000-900 BCE. The other major sources came later—J, 950-800; E, 850-750; P, 700-500; and others up until 400 BCE. It is thought that the Hebrew Bible (Old Testament) as we know it was assembled by an inspired editor around 450-400 BCE. At any rate, the Joseph portion of Genesis is rich with meaning for us as we seek to understand our call.

Actually, it is more than our "call" that is involved. It is not necessarily one call. It is better understood as a life walking with God in such a way that there are ongoing major callings and also our continual calling to live the full life God calls us to, even as new circumstances may offer new ways to live it out.

Dreams (Read Genesis 37:1-11; 40:1-41:46)

Our childhood remembering of Joseph probably centers

on his dreams and him as an interpreter of dreams. Dreams are an almost forgotten way of getting clues to God's calling to us. While dreams often contain completely random recycling and mixing of things we have thought, felt, or experienced, they can also give us insights to enlighten our awareness about the past, present, and even the future. C.G. Jung wrote that "childhood dreams often foreshadow themes in one's life." Certainly, this was true for Joseph.

Perhaps his mistake was sharing them with brothers who were already jealous of their father's favorite son. You would think we would have learned better over the last 3,000 years, but sadly, some haven't gotten the message. Joseph was set up for abuse by his brothers. They were so enraged that they plotted to kill him. Judah brokered a better "deal" for Joseph by selling him into slavery in a foreign country—Egypt.

In Egypt, Joseph makes lemonade of his situation. His owner, Potiphar saw that "the Lord was with Joseph" as "the Lord caused all he did to prosper in his hands." Potiphar kept giving Joseph more and more responsibility. Things were going great until Potiphar's wife took a liking to Joseph and tried to get him to "lie with her." Joseph resisted, but she grabbed his garment as he fled. She used it to "prove" that Joseph had tried to violate her. Note: the issue was not only that he was accused of trying to make love to her, but that he was a slave doing so, and what's more he was a lowly Hebrew.

Now, the slave Joseph lands in a new imprisonment, jail. Once again, he adjusts and shares his gifts by interpreting the dreams of two of the Pharaoh's servants who also are imprisoned. The interpretations prove to be true, and Pharaoh is intrigued by his Hebrew slave who is so accurate in interpreting dreams. The Pharaoh himself is struggling with dreams about seven thin cows eating seven fat cows and seven thin ears of grain swallowing up seven good ears. Pharaoh believed Joseph's interpretation and guidance for the kingdom to store extra grain on seven good years to be able to draw on these storehouses during the seven lean years. Thereafter, Pharaoh installed Joseph as his number two ruler behind himself, giving him charge of administering all the land of Egypt.

Thus, Joseph's story invites us to realize the possibility of God speaking through dreams. I once heard a psychologist lecture on deja vu. He had studied certain persons for many years. He shared about an actress who frequently felt she was having experiences of deja vu. She shared her dreams with the psychologist and collaborated with him to archive them. They found that it was not the case that she has had an experience previously, but that she had dreamed about something before it happened. Then, when the event she had dreamed about occurred, it seemed like she had lived the experience before. This repeated dozens of times over a decade with a strikingly common correspondence of the dream's details with the event that happened sometimes as much as a year later.

The psychologist theorized that deja vu experiences for all of us are mostly connected with dreams. How could this be? C.G. Jung believed that through dreams we often connect at deeper levels of the psyche within the unconscious mind which is not as limited to time and space. C.G. Jung's theory of the Collective Unconscious described a sharing of stories and myths throughout humanity. As some evidence of this, the study of stories in various cultures identifies many common stories from cultures that had not experienced contact with each other when the stories were created. There are many common fairy tales and mythic stories throughout the world.

While I don't want to go too far in simplistic interpretation and valuing of dreams, I had a personal experience about 25 years ago that caused me to believe that God can speak through dreams. At that time, I had an individual spiritual retreat guided by the Rev. Ron DelBene, an Episcopal priest and spiritual director. During the week I spent in a land-locked travel trailer in the woods behind his house, I saw no one except him and his wife. The first night I was there, at the end of an hour session, he requested that I ask God to give me a dream to guide me as to my purpose there that week. Having a scientific background and being somewhat skeptical, I said something like, "I know we dream each night, but I rarely remember one of them. Further, I'm not sure it is proper to ask and expect God to do my bidding by giving me a dream, just because I ask." Ron patiently just asked me to try it.

I prayed God would give me a dream to guide me as to my purpose there. I had three dreams that night, and each night I was there. I've never had an experience like that in my life. I would wake up from a dream and write several pages in a jour-nal. Then, I'd go back to sleep, wake again, write pages, and then repeat the cycle for the third time. Even more significant is the fact that all the dreams were revelatory for that week and my upcoming life. I became convinced that God can and does speak through dreams.

Again, I don't believe every dream is a communication from God or that all dreams have meaning. But some do.

Callings Even When Dreams seem to be Dashed

So how did Joseph's dreams help him to clarify his call-ing? His dreams told him he was to play a key role in leading and governing in big ways. Yet, what was he to think when he was sold into slavery and then landed unjustly in prison. Was "the Lord truly with him?" He had been faithful like Job, yet his circumstances were not bearing out his dreams. If God was in charge, then it must have been God's will that these horrible things happen to him.

One of the best helps for me in understanding the will of God in a world where "bad things happen to good people" is Leslie Weatherhead's little book, *The Will of God*. We live in a culture that has very simplistic understandings of how God guides things. The popular understanding that everything that happens is "caused" by God. In this view, God "pulls strings and pushes buttons" to make specific things happen. It goes along with a kind of transactional view of our relationship with God. I once had a parishioner ask me in all seriousness if God were judging him because God had not given him a Cadillac. He told me that as I knew, he came to the church every morning and went into the chapel to pray by himself. He said he had been telling God that he needed a new car and that he wanted a Cadillac. (I promise you this actually happened.) He seemed to feel that God could just deliver a new Cadillac to him if God chooses to do so. The fact that God wasn't doing this had the man thinking that God was mad at him.

Here is where Weatherhead's ideas about the will of God come in. In the introduction to the book, Weatherhead tells of walking with a physician whose wife had recently died. The physician began to talk about her death as it being the will of God. They were good friends, so Weatherhead, the physician's pastor, said, "Wait a minute, if her death was God's will, why did you try so hard to fight against God's will to keep her from dying?" Weatherhead began to formulate a more complex understanding of God's will. I believe along with Weatherhead that God has created the world with the possibility of free will rather than a world in which everything is fixed and controlled by God. Even God allows us to go against his will. Of course, there is more peace and fulfillment when we live in harmony with God's will.

Weatherhead's contribution to this book is that it helps us understand God's will on three levels. The first level is God's Intentional Will. God created the world to be in harmony and to be a paradise. Yet, we reject God's call to live in the ways of Eden. Thus, the second level to understanding God's will is that God has a Circumstantial Will. The Circumstantial Will of God has God adjusting to the circumstances that the free will of humans and nature allows. In the salvation story, humanity rejected Eden living by the Law as the way to be holy and Godly. Thus, according to Weatherhead, God created plan B, sent Jesus to reconcile the world to God and God's people to each other. Finally, Weatherhead sees the third level of God's will as God's Ultimate Will. It is the Ultimate Will which will prevail to bring about the Realm of God. God is infinitely patient in God's understanding, wooing, and inviting his creatures and his creation to join God's call for peace, reconciliation, justice, opportunity, and joy for all.

Now back to Joseph. How does the Circumstantial Will concept on the way to God's Ultimate Will apply? I believe we can see this most clearly in that climactic scene near the end of Genesis in chapter 50, especially in 50:19-20. Joseph's brothers were cowering in fear that he would punish them. Instead, Joseph acts as an agent of reconciliation. I believe the best translation is that Joseph said, "Do not be afraid! ...even though you intended me harm, God has used what happened for good."

Joseph helped the Circumstantial Will of God moving toward the Ultimate Will to happen because he joined God in being gracious, used his circumstances to bless Egypt, his family, and indeed that whole part of the world through his faithful stewardship. He could have been vindictive, but he chose reconciliation. This reminds me of the story of an emergency room surgeon who realized that it was his bitter enemy, who had sought to do him great harm, who was lying before him disparately in need of the surgery he could perform at that moment. For a split second, he considered not doing the surgery or not doing it properly. But in an instant, he repositioned himself within his calling to "do no harm" and to "apply, for the benefit of the sick, all measures which are required...." This further reminds me of the quote attributed to John Wesley:

"Do all the good you can, by all the means you can, in all the ways you can, in all the places you can, at all the times you can, to all the people you can, as long as ever you can."

So how will you use the gifts God has given you within the circumstances you are given to be part of moving toward God's Ultimate Will? And, how can we even be motivated to try when we feel beat down? Wayne Oates' book, *Life's Detours,* invites us to look at what seem like roadblocks as detours to find another way. Joseph accepted the detours knowing "the Lord was with him" through it all and joined God in caring for the earth and its people using his gifts within his circumstances.

Hope

So, what difference does it make that Joseph had the dreams? What if he'd never had them? Perhaps he would not have had the hope and the knowledge that God was with him and that he was to do great things and provide crucial leadership and stewardship.

51

Although I have concerns about animal testing, this study is astonishing and worth knowing about. In the 1950s, a Harvard-trained researcher based out of Johns Hopkins named Curt Richter ran some fascinating experiments. He wanted to see how long rats could swim in two different conditions. In the first condition, he simply let them swim as long as they could before they gave up and drowned. They lasted 15 minutes on average.

Then, in the other condition, right before they were about to reach their maximum threshold of 15 minutes, he picked them up and dried them off and let them rest briefly before putting them back in. Guess how long they were able to swim after that quick reprieve. Only a few more minutes? Another 15 minutes? Maybe 30 minutes? Try 60 hours!

After being saved, those little rats swam for an astonishing 240 times longer. Why? How is that possible? Richter said it was because of one very simple thing: HOPE. The rats that had been saved had "seen" a better future. They "knew" there was a chance to survive, so they just kept going and going and going.

Callings are not only about the question of what the calling is, but also, they are about believing that we can accomplish our dreams. Trusting in God and in the dreams God inspires, enables us to trust in the possibility and the feasibility of the dreams.

Further, God is dreaming of the world in which his Ultimate Will becomes reality. God is trusting us to fulfill our part of the dream.

Fulfillment

My son, Jamie, said to me a few years ago, "Dad, my life is better than my dreams!" Oh, that everyone could have that level of dream fulfillment. That level of hitting our dream sweet spot only happens when we are sync with the way God has made us and called us within our circumstances.

"Our hearts are restless, till they rest in thee."

St. Augustine

Reflection Questions

Is there a circumstance in your life that might be leading you toward discerning God's will?

If you answered "yes," what first step could you take to follow God's will in this situation?

CHAPTER SIX

Abraham: Listening to Outside Voices

by Bishop Robert Farr

⁸ By faith Abraham, when called to go to a place he would later receive as his inheritance, obeyed and went, even though he did not know where he was going. ⁹ By faith he made his home in the promised land like a stranger in a foreign country; he lived in tents, as did Isaac and Jacob, who were heirs with him of the same promise. ¹⁰ For he was looking forward to the city with foundations, whose architect and builder is God.

Hebrews 11:8-10 (NIV)

Primer

Looking back, who is someone that has made a lasting impact on the direction of your life's journey?

What unexpected twists and turns have occurred along your journey?

As I consider my call, my thoughts turn to the memories of others who spoke "into" me long before my own realization that I was being called. My guess is that I'm not alone. I believe this happens to many of us. We hear from others what they see in us before we see it in ourselves.

The story of my personal call convinced me that what others saw in me was authentic, a call that began from the outside and relentlessly worked its way in through church, events, and people. Like many of us, I grew up with church. But I needed to move beyond church to find my faith – and beyond that – my life call.

My faith call occurred through the course of events and people I met along the way. The first event that shaped my call was a mission trip.

56

As a teenager growing up in Creighton, Missouri, a little town of about 300, our United Methodist Church (UMC) would have up to 50 folks in attendance on a big day. Sixty percent of those were my relatives. Sixty percent of the kids in the youth group I attended were my cousins. I grew up in a fairly small world.

I was a teenage boy who wasn't gifted academically, but who showed talent on the football field, loved having a good time, and had a car to drive. This combination of football, fun, and a car made me a social kid.

Involved in the youth group at Creighton UMC, I became involved in Conference Council on Youth Ministry (CCYM) and was invited to participate in a youth mission trip to a Native American Reservation just outside of Tulsa, Oklahoma. Led by Paul and Shirley Rendle and Jan Bond, I didn't know more than one or two of the other teens participating. My mother was scared to death that I was going. Once we arrived in Oklahoma, our daily routine was to get up early and head out to the job site riding in the back of a pickup truck. At the job site, we dug foundations and laid cement blocks for houses. In the evenings, we returned to the church in downtown Tulsa to eat supper and participate in devotional time before sleeping on the floor of the church.

This downtown Tulsa church exposed me to a different type of church through the missional work and evening devotional time. It was here that I first realized that there is more to faith than just going to church. Before, life and church were separate from each other, and the purpose of church was only to teach me to be a nice, moral, and good citizen. This first missional experience expanded my horizons and caused my thinking to change. Perhaps there was more to this church thing than just going to church. This mission trip would shape my call.

A couple of years later, I experienced a lay witness mission weekend at my home church. This evangelistic event led by a team of lay persons who came to the church to guide Bible study, devotion, conversation, and worship led to a spiritual experience for me. By the end of the weekend, I began to realize even more so that there was more to church than church. This might have been the first time I heard the words, "Holy Spirit." I don't remember the details of the weekend. I don't remember specifically who was there. I do remember that the experience left a huge impression on me that remains even now, 40 years later. It significantly shaped my call.

As a senior in high school, a third event in my life helped shape my call. I wanted to date a young Baptist woman named Susan. Her mother was deeply Baptist and if you wanted to date her daughter, you must attend some Baptist events. Reluctantly, I decided to attend a Baptist Revival. My mother could not understand why I wanted to go this type of religious service. "Why?" she asked. "You're United Methodist! You don't need any of that!" But during the last hymn of that revival service, I found myself at the altar giving my life to Jesus. It seems that it was necessary as a part of my faith experience even though my United Methodist upbringing (and my mother) argued against it. That moment was a touch-point in my life that went beyond my confirmation vows made at church several years earlier. Even today, I extend an invitation at the end of my services because it offers an opportunity for those who hear a calling to answer it and become closer to Jesus.

My call was deeply shaped by The Creighton United Methodist Church, and all that it was and wasn't. The youth rang the church bell, took up the offering and were allowed to paint the youth room any way they wished. The people at

Creighton UMC accepted and loved me. I knew that no matter what happened during the week, no matter how ornery I was, how much trouble I got into, how reckless I acted, for some reason... at 9 o'clock Sunday morning, they did not care about my shortcomings. In fact, the people at Creighton UMC always encouraged me to be somebody regardless of my less than stellar academic performance and teenage angst.

My involvement in the Creighton youth group and CCYM (Conference Council on Youth Ministry) allowed my participation in Annual Conference. I was elected to deliver the youth report at Annual Conference the summer of my senior year. I never knew how that assignment would impact my future.

The Annual Conference gave me the opportunity to meet other preachers who influenced my life through district and conference activities and encouraged me to go to college; a plan I had not considered because of my academic performance in high school. I had planned to follow in the footsteps of my father and become a firefighter. Instead, I enrolled and was accepted at Missouri Western College at St. Joseph, Missouri. In addition, one of my conference connections offered me a part-time paid position as Youth Director at Hyde Valley United Methodist in St. Joseph.

One Friday in February 1978, during my second semester of college, I received a call from the Nevada District Superintendent, Rev. Ross Fulton, Sr. He needed someone to fill in to preach at the Daugherty United Methodist Church southeast of Harrisonville, Missouri. My response? "What would I say?" He replied, "Just give the speech you gave at Annual Conference. I'll give you $25." So, that Sunday, I drove to Daugherty and delivered my conference speech in front of twelve people. Monday morning, I drove back to St. Joe and college.

Later that week, Ross called again and asked if I would

fill in the next Sunday. I responded, "What would you have me say this time? I just gave my speech from conference last week." His response, "Just ask your pastor to help you."

Rev. Ron White, who was serving as a student pastor at the Garden City/Creighton Charge was my pastor and helped me put together a sermon for my next Sunday at Daugherty.

Ross called me two more Fridays in a row and asked me to serve at Daugherty. By the end of the month, he said, "Why don't you finish this up until Annual Conference?" So, I did.

In this process, I began to get confirmation that this was my call. I started to show up for other things at that church. Being a social kid went over well in a small congregation, and by the next Annual Conference, we were running about 30 in worship attendance at this small open country church.

At Annual Conference that year, Ross asked if I would take the Daugherty church as an appointment for the next year. Before I made my decision and during the conference, I was approached by six different pastors. Each one in their own way asked me, "Why don't you consider being a pastor?" I laughed at their suggestion. Being a pastor meant I would have to go all the way through college and go on to get my master's degree. There was no way this was going to happen! They suggested, "Why don't you just try it this year and see...."

I don't know if Ross orchestrated these conversations, but by the end of Annual Conference, I was assigned to Daugherty and signed up for Local Pastor School, a requirement to become a local pastor.

It was in that place I received the final confirmation to my call. Finally, I GOT what everyone else had been speaking into my life. I transferred from Missouri Western to the University of Central Missouri at Warrensburg and pastored Daugherty for the next three years. I learned more about church, life, and people in those three years than almost any other time since. I grew more in faith in those three years than I could imagine. It reminds me of John Wesley's quote, "Preach it until you get it."

So, what does this have to do with Abraham?

Abram was basically set on where his life was going. He had settled along a river. A successful farmer, he owned live-stock and was surrounded by his family and friends. Then, God asked him to take on a whole new direction. This change was so drastic that he changed his name from Abram to Abra-ham. (A Jewish tradition that marked a significant change in an individual's life.)

Verse One in Genesis 12, has been the story of my life.

The Lord had said to Abram, "Go from your country, your people and your father's household to the land I will show you."

Genesis 12:1 (NIV)

At eighteen, if you had asked me where I was going, I would have answered that I was going to be a firefighter as my father before me. I was going to live in the area I grew up in; like most of my family before me. I grew up in the house that my mother grew up in; that her mother grew up in; that her mother grew up in. I would attend the Creighton church, the church that my great-great-grandmother and her sisters planted many years before.

But, like Abraham, I felt called to leave the home I knew and do something completely different. So much, that when I graduated from college, rather than attending St. Paul's in Kansas City (only 45 minutes from home), and under the advisement of Ross (plus $200 travel money), I drove down to Dallas, Texas just "to see what I thought" of Perkins School of Theology. I had never been to Texas in my life. I was met by a District Superintendent from the area who took me to Perkins to look things over, and who had an appointment for me should I move to Texas.

The next thing I knew, I was enrolled in Perkins School of Theology and appointed as an associate pastor at Wesley United Methodist at Greenville, TX. Had I been left to my own devices, I would have remained in Cass County, become a fire-fighter and never finished college.

In my years of ministry and at each new appointment I have received, my first sermon has always included this same line from Genesis.

> [1] **GOD told Abram: "Leave your country, your family, and your father's home for a land that I will show you."**
>
> Genesis 12:1 (NIV)

It has been my call story at every turn.

There was one moment in my first year of seminary in Texas that might have derailed my calling to ministry. In late fall, my grandmother called to let me know that my father had been killed while fighting a fire in Creighton. This was the lone-liest call I have ever received in my life. I was 22. My dad was only 46, and we did not have the best relationship at the time.

Two things happened: I experienced the great hospitality of my church at Greenville. These folks didn't yet really know me. But, they arranged air travel for Susan and I (by this time we were married) back to Missouri. A couple from the church traveled with us because Susan and I had never flown before. They also rented a car and drove us from the airport to Creighton. Then they got a hotel so they could stay with us for the funeral. My pastor and his wife also came up for the funeral. These acts of love I have never forgotten.

At my father's funeral in the Creighton United Methodist Church, I knelt at the rail and asked God, "Is this really what you want me to do? Or, do I just need to go be a firefighter to honor my father?" It was the first time I felt that God spoke to my heart. In my grief, God gave me my call that led me to continue work as a volunteer firefighter and eventually a fire service chaplain for 30 years.

No one had ever spoken into my father's life to tell him that God loved him and needed him in the church. My father always felt that God was mean and didn't like blue collar men like himself. This has led me over my 40 years as a minister to emphasize reaching new people who are outside the walls of the church.

As I think about my call story, I think about how the Holy Spirit has influenced my journey. Rather than the flash of lightning or the clap of thunder that others have experienced, my journey has been more about the nudging of the Holy Spirit and learning how to learn to look for and listen to that nudge. The nudge to... make a phone call, visit someone in the hospital, try something new, or in this case, answer my call to ministry. I will be the first to admit that I probably missed a great percentage of the Holy Spirit's nudging. It is a continual struggle to leave enough time or space so that the Holy Spirit's nudging doesn't get overrun by the daily demands and struggles of life.

The moral of my call story is this; it is important to listen to other people to find your own voice and your own call. To this day, I'm always asking people, "Have you considered, have you thought about being a pastor?" If someone hadn't done that for me, I wouldn't be here. Receive the voice of others, and be the voice for others. It is my hope that the average person who thinks, "I can't do this," will read this story and think instead, "If he can do this, so can I!"

Reflection Questions

Who are you investing in?

Can you think of a person or two you should be asking about their call?

Who is somebody to whom you speak an encouraging word?

Where have you missed or ignored somebody's voice speaking to you?

CHAPTER SEVEN

Servant Girl: Called by God

by Bishop Debra Wallace-Padgett

¹ Now Naaman was commander of the army of the king of Aram. He was a great man in the sight of his master and highly regarded, because through him the Lord had given victory to Aram. He was a valiant soldier, but he had leprosy.[a]

² Now bands of raiders from Aram had gone out and had taken captive a young girl from Israel, and she served Naaman's wife. ³ She said to her mistress, "If only my master would see the prophet who is in Samaria! He would cure him of his leprosy."

⁴ Naaman went to his master and told him what the girl from Israel had said. 5 "By all means, go," the king of Aram replied. "I will send a letter to the king of Israel." So Naaman left, taking with him ten talents[b] of silver, six thousand shekels[c] of gold and ten sets of clothing. ⁶ The letter that he took to the king of Israel read: "With this letter I am sending my servant Naaman to you so that you may cure him of his leprosy."

⁷ As soon as the king of Israel read the letter, he tore his robes and said, "Am I God? Can I kill and bring back to life? Why does this fellow send someone to me to be cured of his leprosy? See how he is trying to pick a quarrel with me!"

⁸ When Elisha the man of God heard that the king of Israel had torn his robes, he sent him this message: "Why have you torn your robes? Have the man come to me and he will know that there is a prophet in Israel." ⁹ So Naaman went with his horses and chariots and stopped at the door of Elisha's house. ¹⁰ Elisha sent a messenger to say to him, "Go, wash yourself seven times in the Jordan, and your flesh will be restored and you will be cleansed."

II Kings 5:1-10 (NIV)

Primer

Think of someone you have met who has been called by God for a certain task.

How did you first recognize this person was called by God?

Each one of us is called to service by God. Not just those who become pastors, missionaries, or full-time church staff members, but every person who lives on this earth. We can deny, reject, or even miss hearing the call, yet the call comes to each of us. We answer with "yes," "no," or "maybe later."

Several persons answer God's call affirmatively in II Kings 5:1-10:

1) Naaman experiences transformation in his life.

2) Elisha is a conduit through whom God works to bring healing to Naaman.

3) Naaman's wife serves as a catalyst to her husband of the good news of hope for his healing.

However, that is not the whole story. There is an unlikely person who becomes a major player in the plot. She is akin to the understudy at the Opera House who steps up when the star is ill and performs with more giftedness than anyone expects or the player who barely made the team cut entering the baseball game in the bottom of the ninth and hitting a grand slam home run.

There are those times in life when someone makes an unexpected appearance on the stage and brings down the house. No one would have expected Naaman's wife's young servant girl to answer God's call on her life. She is not one of the big names in the Bible. Indeed, her name is not even mentioned in Scripture. She is a Jewish girl captured in war by the Arameans.

She is a nobody who has lost her homeland and freedom, but has not lost her faith. Indeed, she gladly talks about her faith with Naaman's wife. The result of her actions changes history. More importantly to the Army Commander Naaman – it changes his life.

And it all happens because the servant girl answers God's call to share her faith.

Faith-sharing is at the heart of what it means to be a Christ-follower. How else can we fulfill Jesus' parting instructions to his disciples?

"Go therefore and make disciples…"

(Matthew 28:16 ff) (NIV)

How else can we live out the mission stated with such clarity in The United Methodist Book of Discipline?

"The mission of the church is to make disciples of Jesus Christ for the transformation of the world."

How else does a United Methodist conference like my own embody its vision?

"Spiritual leaders empowering life-giving congregations to transform the world."

Talking about our faith is part of the Christian lifestyle. Yet faith-sharing is something that many of us struggle to do. Perhaps we are concerned that we will come across as pushy. Or maybe we think that our words are inadequate. Perhaps there is another reason that prevents us from sharing with others the best news that this world has ever known.

If this is your situation, know that you are not alone. According to recent Barna research, the vast majority of Christ-followers have not shared our faith with a non-Christian in the past year. That does not give us an out on faith-sharing, though. It is at the core of the Christian life. Not only does faith-sharing potentially help others, it also helps us grow in our Christian walk. Indeed, it is good for our souls.

Some of us may struggle with faith-sharing. But the servant girl in today's Scripture passage has no difficulty with it. When the time is right, she willingly shares with Naaman's wife the Good News of Yahweh God who means so much to her and her people. She is like my mother who called me recently with the news of my niece's pregnancy. The news of becoming a great-grandmother was too good for Mom to keep to herself. So is the news the servant girl has of what Yahweh can do in Naaman's life.

A wonderful lesson about faith-sharing is highlighted in today's Scripture passage. What the servant girl says is not nearly as significant as who she is. She is the real deal, an authentic follower of God. Her authenticity plays itself out in two ways.

First, she has authentic compassion for Naaman, his wife, and the difficulties that they face in life. Granted, Naaman has a lot going for him. He is the highly respected, powerful and successful commander of a large Aramean army.

But he has leprosy, a health problem that money and power cannot fix. In the ancient world, leprosy referred to a variety of skin ailments, some of which were fatal and all which were considered highly contagious. Though Naaman is held in high regard by the leaders of his country, his illness causes him to be relegated to the "unclean" category. Nobody wants to be around him for fear that they will catch his disease. Surely Naaman notices the long stares and whispers behind his back. What he would give to be healed!

But all of the medical expertise of that day and all of the money in the world cannot eradicate Naaman's health situation. He learns to live with it, hoping that it will not eventually kill him. Living with a serious illness is not easy for anyone. It is especially hard for someone as accustomed to finding solutions to problems as Naaman.

The servant girl undoubtedly realizes how sad it makes Naaman and his wife to deal with his leprosy. Maybe she has caught a glimpse of Naaman's wife wiping away an unexpected tear at an inopportune time. Perhaps she notices Naaman's wistful look or occasional sigh. Regardless, she feels compassion for Naaman and his wife, wanting life to be better for them. She longs for them to know healing from God's hand. She waits for the opportunity to introduce them to her God, Yahweh. She does not have an agenda or goals in her sharing. She simply shares her faith because she authentically cares.

Others can tell whether or not our care for them is authentic. This is illustrated beautifully in *Same Kind of Different as*

Me, a true story about two persons from extreme opposite life experiences.

Ron is a successful businessman. Denver is a street person. They are brought together by Ron's wife, Debra, who has a heart for the homeless. Ron and Denver exchange multiple insights. Sometimes Ron, the businessman, is the teacher. More often, Denver, the street person, is the one with a wise word. My favorite section of the book describes Denver asking Ron about a fishing technique called "catch and release" in which fishers throw fish they catch back in the water instead of keeping them to eat and enjoy.

> **"So, Mr. Ron, it occurred to me: If you is fishin for a friend you just gon' catch and release, then I ain't got no desire to be your friend."**

A little further down, he completes his thought:

> **"But if you is lookin for a real friend, then I'll be one. Forever."**
>
> **Same Kind of Different as Me**
> *Ron Hall and Denver Moore*

When our compassion is authentic, we are not interested in "catch and release" relationships. We do not reach out to others just so that we will feel better about ourselves or to add new members to our church or to check off a to-do in the discipleship box. We reach out to others because we know that God cares about them. This is the primary reason that we show we care.

How compassionate are you and I for persons we know who are living without God? For persons who have not experienced a relationship with Jesus Christ? Do we care? Do we really care?

I appreciate a friend's frequent prayer in recent years. He

71

says, "I pray that God will break my heart for persons who do not have Christ in their lives."

That kind of heart is what drives us to tell others about how Jesus is working in our lives. It is what gives us the humility to share our personal before-Christ and after-Christ stories. It is what causes us to be willing to discuss the struggles we have in our lives. If we do not have that kind of heart, then it is good and right for us to ask God to change us, to request that God give us a heart which truly cares for other people.

There is more to faith-sharing than authentic compassion, though. We must also have an authentic personal faith. The servant girl has a deep faith. She knows of Elisha and the work God does through him. She believes with all of her heart that Elisha can help her master. She says to her mistress, "If only my lord were with the prophet who is in Samaria! He would cure him of his leprosy" (II Kings 10:3). She shares her faith because she **has** faith.

One of my favorite lines about faith-sharing comes from Bishop Dick Wills' book, *Waking to God's Dream*. Bishop Wills writes, "You cannot share what you do not have." This truth was driven home to me one afternoon years ago when I was shooting some basketball hoops with friends. We were simply passing the time enjoying being together. Then one friend began giving me "tips" on my jump shot, which had been my signature shot when playing small college basketball. Now there is no question that I could improve my jump shot. But this friend did not even have a jump shot. The bottom line is that I did not receive his suggestions well. Oh, I smiled and thanked him for his input. However, I wondered from whence he thought his authority on basketball came. I had not read Wills' book at the time. But I knew firsthand the truth of its thesis, "You cannot share what you do not have."

You cannot teach someone how to improve their jump shot if you do not have one yourself. More importantly, you cannot share the vibrancy of the Christian faith if your faith is not alive and well. You cannot speak convincingly of the life-changing power of Jesus Christ unless you have experienced it firsthand. You cannot share your faith unless you have one.

Conversely, when we do have faith, we are called to share it. Our age, ethnicity, gender or station in life does not change this call. How a person looks or what they say is much less significant than who they are. Sharing our faith starts with an authentic compassion for others. It also requires that we **have** a faith.

Answering God's call to share our faith just might change someone's life. It will certainly change ours.

Reflection Questions

How important do you think it is to share your faith with others?

Describe a time when you have either received or offered "catch and release" faith sharing.

What does it mean to have a heart broken for those who do not know Christ?

How do you respond to Bishop Dick Wills' statement, "You cannot share what you do not have?"

CHAPTER EIGHT

Philip: Helping People Discover Jesus

by Phil Maynard

[43] The next day Jesus decided to leave for Galilee. Finding Philip, he said to him, "Follow me." [44] Philip, like Andrew and Peter, was from the town of Bethsaida. [45] Philip found Nathanael and told him, "We have found the one Moses wrote about in the Law, and about whom the prophets also wrote—Jesus of Nazareth, the son of Joseph." [46] "Nazareth! Can anything good come from there?" Nathanael asked. "Come and see," said Philip.

John 1:43-46 (NIV)

Primer

Have you ever felt like you were directly selected by God to carry out an assignment?

How would you define "disciple of Christ?"

He wasn't the leader of a church of thousands, although he did ask Jesus how he could feed the multitudes gathered to hear the Master teach. He came from the small town of Bethsaida, rather than a metropolis like Jerusalem, and spent most of his ministry in a rural setting. He wasn't the first to be asked to follow Jesus. In fact, he was halfway down the roster of the original twelve in order of call. He wasn't even part of the inner circle—the nucleus within the twelve that would catalyze a moment that turned the world upside down.

Like most of us receiving a call to ministry, Philip was an ordinary person.

Yet his calling was anything but ordinary.

My favorite mention of Philip from the gospels is the narrative from John 1:43-51. It is an example of a threefold pattern that repeats itself in the brief biblical references to Philip: Respond-Follow-Witness.

The account from the first chapter of John begins with the invitation. It was an invitation directly from Jesus. Not all the disciples had this direct invitation from Jesus himself. In fact, most were brought to Jesus by another disciple.

Recognizing this invitation is the starting point of understanding our own call. Just as it was for Philip, our call is to follow Jesus. There is a lot of conversation these days about what it means to "follow Jesus." Most of us have grown up with a language that equates the word disciple with the word learner. While disciples are definitely learners, this is a limited understanding of the life of discipleship. Discipleship is not about memorizing facts and stories involving Jesus or learning about what life could look like if we followed Jesus' principles. Discipleship is about becoming like Jesus. It is not about information. It's about transformation. It is not about knowledge. It's about behaviors.

Discipleship in the time of Jesus meant leaving everything behind to literally follow the Rabbi (the Teacher). It was a great honor to be called, and there was no greater aspiration than to become like the teacher.

Philip made such a commitment to follow Jesus—to become a disciple.

However, discipleship moves beyond the moment of affirming allegiance. It is about followership. Philip left his former life behind to go and follow Jesus. We don't know a lot about his previous life. He had a Greek name, and at one point in the Gospel account, he introduces some Greek people to Jesus, so there is some speculation that Philip was a 'connector' to the Greek community from the ministry of Jesus. In the story about the feeding of the multitudes in John's version of the Sermon on the Mount, Jesus asks Philip where to buy bread. It is a test; one that Philip fails. Jesus already knows how he is going to feed the multitudes.

Yet Philip continues to stumble along in well-meaning faith. When some Greeks came to see Jesus, Philip enlists the help of Andrew and gets them an audience. But it is also Philip who, later, still doesn't get it. As Jesus gives final instructions to the disciples, Philip pleads, "Lord, show us the Father and that will be enough for us." To which Jesus responds, "Anyone who has seen me has seen the Father" (John 14:9).

The thing that Philip did get, however, and at which he excelled, was the Witness dimension of his calling.

There is something about meeting Jesus that is life transforming in a way that makes us eager to share the good news. We see this pattern over and over again in the New Testament:

•The shepherds who went to Bethlehem and found the baby Jesus immediately "spread the word concerning what had been told them about this child, and all who heard it were amazed. . ." (Luke 2:17-18).

• The first thing Andrew did following his invitation to follow Jesus was to find his brother Simon Peter and "he brought him to Jesus" (John 1:42).

• The first thing Philip did after responding to the call to follow Jesus was to find Nathanael and share the good news: "We have found the one Moses wrote about in the law . . . Jesus of Nazareth. . . . Come and see" (John 1:44-46).

Philip's story is a great witness not only to the calling to respond-follow-witness. It points us in the direction of the unique focus of those called to the ministry of leading people to discover Jesus. In this instance, it was Philip inviting Nathanael to meet Jesus.

Note Nathanael's response: "Nazareth? Can anything good come from there?"

Substitute the word "church" for "Nazareth" and you have the exact question being asked by the culture we are called to reach with the good news: "Church? Can anything good come from there?"

And yet, it is precisely through the Church that those called to the unique role of Pastor find themselves operating. In the midst of developing programs and leading worship, organizing staff and maintaining buildings, visiting the sick and counseling those who struggle, and managing a budget and leading mission trips, the central call remains to introduce people to Jesus and equip the congregation with tools to introduce people to Jesus.

When we do this well, the answer to Nathanael's question and the question of our culture (Can anything good come from the church?) becomes, "Yes . . . Jesus."

The call to ministry is not about embarking on a career or building a professional resume of ever-larger churches served. It is about the holy work of introducing people to Jesus:

• Developing your own relationship with Jesus through the practice of spiritual disciplines and growing toward maturity as a disciple in the ways of life.

• Being present to people outside the church so that they see the love of Jesus through your life and are invited to discover God's love for themselves.

• Equipping disciples to engage people outside the church so that they may meaningfully give of themselves to others.

• Training disciples to share their stories and experiences with Jesus so that others may be invited to find their own stories and experiences.

• Creating a culture where helping people discover a new and abundant life in Jesus is more important than all the things we might do to create beautiful spaces and great programs.

In the United Methodist Church, we capture the essence of these ideas through a succinct mission statement: Make disciples of Jesus Christ for the transformation of the world.

If we are not focused on the work of introducing people to Jesus, we can't fulfill this mission or answer Jesus' clear call: "Go, therefore (literally "as you go") and make disciples. . . ." (Mathew 28:19).

Sadly, despite the clarity of this call, a significant majority of mainline denominational churches go year after year without a single new person coming to a relationship with Jesus. We've met our budgets, maintained our buildings, conducted our Sunday School classes, had our potluck dinners, and even sponsored mission trips. Still, nobody seems to have met Jesus.

There are lots of organizations and clubs and agencies that do good things for people. They raise a lot of money, collect supplies, offer care and comfort, and sometimes even address the systemic issues that underlie the need for these services. Rather, there is only one body that introduces people to Jesus—the Church.

Philip models this basic calling of all disciples, all congregations, and the Church—to connect people to the Savior—in the moment he introduces Nathanael to Jesus. It is our calling.

Let's keep the main thing the main thing. Help people meet

Jesus! That is what will make your calling extraordinary.

Reflection Questions

Did someone introduce you to Jesus?

Can you remember a time when you introduced someone to Jesus?

Is there someone God is calling on you to introduce to Jesus?

CHAPTER NINE

Esther: A Jewish Queen

by Julie Blackwelder Holly

[14b] "And who knows but that you have come to your royal position for such a time as this?"

Esther 3:14b (NIV)

Primer

Have you ever found it necessary to take on a role in which you didn't feel qualified? If you did, how did you handle the situation?

Who is someone in your life who has exhibited great courage?

Read Esther 3:1-14 and 4:1-16

On the wall by the windows in my office hangs a canvas painted by a young woman from one of the churches I served. She painted these words on the canvas, "Perhaps this is the moment for which you were created." These words are inspired by the story of Esther, a book that celebrates the deliverance of the Jewish community from genocide at the hands of the Persian rulers. God, whose name is found nowhere in the book, saves the people through a young woman named Esther.

Esther did not possess the generally expected qualities of a deliverer and savior. She appeared to be quite the opposite. Esther was an orphan, raised by her cousin, Mordecai. She was a woman in what can only be described as a man's world, making her powerless on her own. It was completely out of her control to alter her fate when King Ahasuerus had his people round her up, along with many other young virgin women for his harem. At first, no one was aware that Esther was also Jewish in a definitively gentile-ruled kingdom, making her part of the religious and political minority.

From all indication, Esther was destined for little beyond a life of subjugation under the authority of men with much more power and autonomy than her. God, however, known through scripture to call on unlikely characters, was not hindered by all that was stacked against Esther. Neither in our lives is God limited by our experience and strengths for the ways in which God calls us to serve. Empowering us in new ways, God calls us sometimes to unexpected roles that run counter to all indicators of where our capabilities lie.

Along the way, Esther found herself in roles she could not have anticipated, considering her social standing and personal history. After being rounded up for the king's purposes, she won the king's favor and became queen. Esther later inadvertently saved the king's life by passing on information to the king about a deadly plot that was overheard by her cousin, Mordecai. A queen. The savior of a king. She could hardly aspire to accomplish more considering her circumstances, and yet Esther found herself in another unexpected position with the opportunity to do something to benefit the entirety of the Jewish community within the kingdom. Her cousin, Mordecai, offended Haman, an influential companion to the king. Haman arranged to gain, through deceit and manipulation, the king's approval for a decree that allowed for all the Jewish people—including Mordecai—to be killed. When Mordecai learned of the plot, he turned to Esther and her position as queen to seek help. Esther, aware of her position of powerlessness and of the rule that anyone approaching the king without being summoned would be killed unless the king pardons them, understandably hesitated. What God was calling Esther to do, through the Jewish people and her cousin in particular, meant revealing the truth about who she was and risking her life. She was called on to summon the courage to take a step into the unknown.

Esther is not alone in this. So many of us feel unworthy, unprepared, and ill-suited when faced with challenges that require great courage and carry significant risk. Scripture teaches us that in these circumstances, we should look to God for help, wisdom, and strength. It is God who will lead us through difficulties and bring us clarity in discernment. God sometimes acts directly, answering prayers with a sign, a word, or direct intervention. At other times, God calls and directs us through the lives and wisdom of other people.

As a college senior, all my post-graduate plans began to fall apart. I was at a loss when people posed THE question asked of all college seniors: "What will you do after graduation?" I kept myself from panicking through regular prayer and the knowledge that my eye doctor would love to have me work as his receptionist again if everything else failed. I would at least have an income, but I wanted more than an income. I wanted a purpose. I just had no idea how to discern it. One day, close to the middle of my senior fall semester, a retired bishop who was teaching part-time at my college requested a meeting with me. Given that I had just recently submitted my first paper for his class, I was not looking forward to hearing what he had to say. He caught me completely off guard when he asked me point blank whether

I had ever considered pastoral ministry and then expressed his belief that God was calling me to ordained ministry. I believed him to be misled. However, I agreed to prayerfully reflect on this possibility because of my understanding of God's ability to speak to us through the wisdom of other people.

In Esther's actions, we find a reflection of the wisdom in Proverbs 12:15. "Fools think their own way is right, but the wise listen to advice." Esther, despite her own great anxiety and hesitancy to act, relied on both God and the community of faith. Not clear of her calling to serve God in this circumstance, she trusted the wisdom of Mordecai. She also sought out God's direction and protection, dedicating time to prayer and fasting before God. She asked her friends in the palace, her cousin, and the whole Jewish community in Susa to pray and fast with her, appealing to God—we may assume—for wisdom, courage, and deliverance. This portion of Esther's story testifies to the value of the worshiping community. Coming together for a single purpose, the Jewish people communicated God's power and presence with Esther. Carrying the knowledge that we are not alone in our discernment of God's way and call for our life provides a particular reassurance that we cannot possess on our own.

Through God's grace and Esther's careful cunningness, the king acted to empower the Jewish community to defend themselves against any attackers attempting to destroy them. Haman and his co-conspirators were killed on the gallows he had fashioned for Mordecai. Esther, in the style of the judges, became a celebrated deliver and savior of God's people. In true-to-life fashion, this story does not conclude with a perfect, holy, and happy ending for all. For Esther, at least, she discovered that despite all the factors set against her, she could—with God's help and the support of the community of faith— exercise leadership and use what gifts she had to help others and to serve God. In essence, this is God's call for all of us—to love and serve God and neighbor . However, the question for each of us revolves around the way in which God calls us to fulfill these greatest of the commandments. We are each created and called to work with God in the world, in large and small ways, for God's reconciling and redemptive purpose and to respond faithfully when we discern God's specific call for us.

Similar to Esther, my instinct in the face of God's call was hesitation and uncertainty. I was a 22-year-old young woman called to ordained ministry in a world that still sometimes sees femaleness as a disqualifying factor. Strangers, a couple family members, and friends declared my calling, and even my intention to attend seminary, as unbiblical. I did not possess the clarity to clearly articulate the particular call that was developing in my life and felt ill-equipped to fully respond. As I continued to pray and seek God's way, though, doors of opportunity opened and the voice of the community of faith grew in volume and consistency in affirming my gifts for and calling to ministry. Even in my hesitation and uncertainty, God led me to faithfully, though gradually, respond.

God's call in our lives is not limited to a single circumstance. We all have the opportunity to receive God's call to an overarching purpose or vocation that carries over all through our lives. We may think that once we have successfully discerned this larger call that our work is done. On the contrary, discerning God's call in our lives involves daily intentionality as we seek our place and our voice in each situation we encounter. From Esther, we learn that we cannot always discern God's call by ourselves. When we fail to see where God is calling us, let us seek the wisdom of God through prayer, scripture, and worship; and the wisdom of the community of faith through faithful listening, service, and fellowship. Only then may we discover the calling for which we were created.

Reflection Questions

What do you understand to be your limitations to serving God? In what circumstances have you been able to overcome them?

Make a list of your gifts and strengths. How could you use these to serve God and neighbor ?

Who are the trusted and wise people in your community of faith who can pray for your discernment and provide honest feedback about your gifts?

Spend some time reading through the book of Proverbs. What wisdom do you find that is particularly connected with your current circumstances?

In what ways have you experienced smaller, more circumstantial callings? Were there any common elements in these calls of God? Consider which of your gifts you used to respond. Could these more specific experiences of call help you discern God's larger calling in your life?

CHAPTER TEN

Mary: Mary Said Yes

by Bishop Debra Wallace-Padgett

[26] In the sixth month of Elizabeth's pregnancy, God sent the angel Gabriel to Nazareth, a town in Galilee, [27] to a virgin pledged to be married to a man named Joseph, a descendant of David. The virgin's name was Mary. [28] The angel went to her and said, "Greetings, you who are highly favored! The Lord is with you." [29] Mary was greatly troubled at his words and wondered what kind of greeting this might be. [30] But the angel said to her, "Do not be afraid, Mary; you have found favor with God. [31] You will conceive and give birth to a son, and you are to call him Jesus. [32] He will be great and will be called the Son of the Most High. The Lord God will give him the throne of his father David, [33] and he will reign over Jacob's descendants forever; his kingdom will never end."

[34] "How will this be," Mary asked the angel, "since I am a virgin?" [35] The angel answered, "The Holy Spirit will come on you, and the power of the Most High will overshadow you. So the holy one to be born will be called [a] the Son of God. [36] Even Elizabeth your relative is going to have a child in her old age, and she who was said to be unable to conceive is in her sixth month. [37] For no word from God will ever fail."

[38] "I am the Lord's servant," Mary answered. "May your word to me be fulfilled." Then the angel left her.

Luke 1:26-38 (NIV)

Primer

Name some people in your life who you sense were called by God.

What causes you to believe they were called by God?

[1]In those days Caesar Augustus issued a decree that a census should be taken of the entire Roman world. [2] (This was the first census that took place while Quirinius was governor of Syria). [3] And everyone went to their own town to register.

[4] So Joseph also went up from the town of Nazareth in Galilee to Judea, to Bethlehem the town of David, because he belonged to the house and line of David. [5] He went there to register with Mary, who was pledged to be married to him and was expecting a child. [6] While they were there, the time came for the baby to be born, [7] and she gave birth to her firstborn, a son. She wrapped him in cloths and placed him in a manger, because there was no guest room available for them.

Luke 2:1-7 (NIV)

God's call comes to us in a variety of ways. For some of us, it unfolds over time. This describes my experience of God's call which first surfaced at my baptism as I professed my faith and committed my life as a Christ-follower. Numerous "next steps" followed, including years of service as a layperson, consecration as a diaconal minister, additional education, 11 years as a staff person in a large church, ordination, pastoring, appointment as a district superintendent, and eventually consecration as a bishop.

I certainly did not see the road map in the beginning. I am glad I did not as it probably would have overwhelmed me! But looking back, I recognize that God called me through each transition along the way.

Other people experience God's call in more dramatic ways. Take Rev. Marshall Eugene Powell, the father of one of my close friends. Eugene was a 26-year-old Korean War veteran, living on a farm in Western Kentucky. As he went out one morning to milk his cow, he heard an audible voice behind him say, "You have always thought of yourself as a personal worker."

He turned around to discover that no one was there. He then turned back to go to the cow and heard a voice inside him say, "Do you remember when you were going overseas, how you wished you could tell the scared guys about a friend who sticks closer than a brother?"

"Sure," answered Eugene.

"Why couldn't you talk to them as one since they were all dressed the same and all afraid to go to Korea?"

"Yes. What are you trying to tell me? Are you trying to tell me that I need to go into the ministry?" (He thought he might become an army chaplain).

The inward voice continued, "You get the point."

Eugene went into the house and told his wife that he thought he had been called to preach. She said, "I knew it! I wondered when you were going to find it out."

God's call to Mary, the mother of Jesus, was even more dramatic. Indeed, you could say that God sent heaven down to Mary in calling her to service centuries ago. That's right – heaven came to earth in the birth of Jesus Christ that first Christmas.

What does one do in response to a call like that? Luke 2 provides an answer to this question.

Mary is a young teenager. She will soon marry her fiancée, Joseph, and they will start a family together. Joseph is a catch in many ways. In addition to having a reputable vocation as a carpenter, he can trace his ancestral roots all the way back to King David, the greatest military leader Israel has ever known. The future looks bright for Mary and Joseph.

Then one ordinary day Mary has a visit from God that changes her life forever. The scriptures do not tell us what she is doing when the angel comes to her. Perhaps she has just awakened and is getting ready to go downstairs and start breakfast. Or maybe she is enjoying a devotional time with God. For that matter, she might be taking a break after a long day of hard work. Regardless, heaven comes down to Mary in that moment.

God comes to us in ordinary moments as well. You may feel that you are in an ordinary time in your life right now. You are living at a humdrum pace. Your days seem insignificant. You go to school like you have for years. Maybe the excitement of your job has worn off. Though life is fine in many ways, it feels stale to you. You sometimes wonder if there is not more to it than what you are currently experiencing. Everything feels so ordinary.

This particular day may have begun as an ordinary day to Mary, but it turns out to be extraordinary. Heaven comes to Mary when an angel begins a conversation with her.

> [29] Mary was greatly troubled at his words and wondered what kind of greeting this might be. [30] But the angel said to her, "Do not be afraid, Mary; you have found favor with God.
>
> Luke 1:29-30 (NIV)

Our encounters with God may frighten us, too. Most of us do not have conversations with angels from heaven. Indeed, our communication with God might not seem supernatural at all. Perhaps God speaks to us through a tug at our heart or a Word of Scripture. Maybe it's through dialogue with another person. Nevertheless, God comes to us, and sometimes God's Word to us is frightening.

Ask Rob and Susie who are led to leave their secure jobs in the U.S. and travel to another country for a six-year tour as missionaries. Ask the teenager who senses God calling him to reach out to a lonely new student at school. Ask the mom who is courageously refusing to enable her adult child in his addictions. Ask the church that is on the verge of taking a huge step of faith in expanding their ministries.

The angel begins to explain to Mary that she has nothing to fear. She is not the one in charge of making this happen. God is pleased with her and will work out the details of the plan. It seems impossible to her, but all will work out exactly as it should, and the outcome will be greater than she can imagine.

> [31] You will conceive and give birth to a son, and you are to call him Jesus. [32] He will be great and will be called the Son of the Most High. The Lord God will give him the throne of his father David.
>
> (Luke 1:31-32) (NIV)

That brings us to Mary's response to God. Heaven has come down for Mary. She has heard God's call on her life. She does not understand why or how or even the full implications of this reality. Even so, she has heard enough to formulate her answer to God's call.

> [38] **"I am the Lord's servant," Mary answered. "May your word to me be fulfilled." Then the angel left her.**
>
> Luke 1:38 (NIV)

We say "yes" to God when we find the time to spend with Jesus Christ on a daily basis, when we offer a helping hand, when we look for ways to make it easier for someone overwhelmed with life and when we support a need that is significant.

We say "yes" to God when we contribute to our church's ministries with time, talent, and monies, or accept another person as they are, instead of conditionally. We say "yes" to God when we take time to stop and show that we care, when we affirm and encourage not only the children close to us but also that child who doesn't ever seem to have anyone at the ballpark or the orchestra concerts to support them. We say "yes" to God when we carefully look at our time commitments and reorganize them according to God's values.

We say "yes" to God when we care enough about another person to pray for them regularly. A "yes" to God is whispered when someone finally acknowledges the addiction that is destroying them and their family and enters a treatment center. There are many ways to say "yes" to God.

After Mary says yes to God, the Scripture passage concludes with these words. "The angel left her." The rest of Luke's Gospel describes how the world is different from that moment forward. And it all starts with a "yes" from a young Jewish girl who lives in first century Israel.

Heaven came down, and God called Mary to service. When she said "yes" to God's call for her to be the mother of the Savior of the world, she was changed forever. Our "yes" to God has a lasting impact upon us as well, affecting us for the rest of our lives.

The physical changes Mary experiences during her pregnancy are simply a prelude to all that follows after the baby Jesus arrives. Her capacity to love is expanded when she holds her newborn in her arms. Her priorities shift when Christ becomes the center of her life. Her life is transformed after she says "yes" to God's call.

When we say "yes" to God's call on our lives, we are also changed. As God takes center place in our lives, we become different people. This is what God asks of you and me. God wants first place in our lives. God wants to be as central to us as newborn babies are to their parents. God wants us to share the news of Jesus' coming with others. When we do, our lives are transformed.

Heaven is here, friends. God has come to us, calling us to serve. We can say "no" to the invitation. After all, God leaves the choice up to us. We can also choose to say "yes." If we do, we can be certain that our lives will be changed forever!

Heaven came down to Mary, and God called her to serve in new ways. She answered with a resounding "Yes!" that changed the history of the world. Heaven has come to us, too, as God calls us to deepened service. How will we respond?

Reflection Questions

Has God's call on your life been revealed slowly over time, in a dramatic moment or both? Describe.

When heaven came down to Mary, she said yes to God. Describe the most recent time when you have said yes to God.

Mary's yes to God changed her life forever. How has your yes to God transformed your life?

Name one way in which God is calling you to deepened service.

CHAPTER ELEVEN

Jonah: He Knew God's Voice

by Jacob Reedy

¹ The word of the Lord came to Jonah son of Amittai: ² "Go to the great city of Nineveh and preach against it, because its wickedness has come up before me."

³ But Jonah ran away from the Lord and headed for Tarshish. He went down to Joppa, where he found a ship bound for that port. After paying the fare, he went aboard and sailed for Tarshish to flee from the Lord.

⁴ Then the Lord sent a great wind on the sea, and such a violent storm arose that the ship threatened to break up.

Jonah 1:1-4 (NIV)

Primer

Can you remember a time when you felt like you were hiding – or keeping a secret – from God?

How would you react if God called you to do something that frightened you?

I have had a very fickle relationship with Jonah. When I was a kid, he was awesome. Getting swallowed by a fish and going on a three-day cruise? Absolutely amazing! As I grew older, I began to learn more about the other animal in the story: the worm.

It's not my intention to shatter any preconceived notions you have about Jonah. If he's your hero, and you think of him as a perfect example of the ideal follower of God, you might want to stop reading now.

Thankfully, in some ways, life is like a river. Many of our views and opinions are akin to stones along the bottom of the water. Then, in time, our views get smoothed as the water rushes onward. How amazing is that it that the views we felt could never coexist, over time have combined in a way to create something breathtakingly beautiful?

It took time for me to start seeing the beauty of Jonah's tale. At first, I wasn't sure it was possible. Most folks reading this book know nothing about me, other than I was asked to write this chapter. However, you can trust me on this. Like much of God's creation, Jonah's story shines brightly before all is said and done.

The first thing that we learn about Jonah is that God talks to Jonah and he recognizes God's voice. There is a relationship here and, at first glance, it seems to be a solid relationship much like a parent and a child.

Take a moment to consider this. Jonah knows God so well that he is surprised to hear God's voice. He recognizes the voice much like a child recognizes a parent's voice, and knows immediately who it is.

We quickly learn that God displays a lot of trust in Jonah by entrusting him with something really important. Trust doesn't come quickly in most relationships. There is something special between God and Jonah.

Is Jonah's reaction to God's call to action the best? Probably not. Imagine if a child turned and ran at a parent's request. It's quite possible the parent would be disappointed, and the child might come to regret the decision to disobey.

On the other hand, doesn't Jonah deserve some measure of credit for actually knowing God is calling him? Absolutely. It's easy to see Jonah's reaction as a rejection of God. Although it wasn't a stellar example of trust, Jonah had no doubt to whom he was reacting.

How many of us have failed to respond to God's call because we never took the time to listen for it? Or, on the other hand, perhaps we've spent so much time trying to figure out if we heard God correctly that we missed an important opportunity. It's easy to do. I would be surprised if there's anyone reading this book that hasn't missed a call from God at some point.

Unlike some, I don't usually enjoy the early stages of a relationship, whether it's a new relationship with a friend, a romantic relationship, or a professional relationship. I feel like there are too many awkward moments as each of us try to figure out this new relationship that is being developed. It is a constant game of trying to say the right thing and trying to understand what the other person is really saying.

With patience and a measure of luck, we can get to a point where guessing is no longer the dominant feature of the relationship. The conversation gets easier and better. Instead of feeling nervous, we eventually relax.

If our relationships with others are miniature models of our relationship with God, then shouldn't we expect some of those awkward moments with God as well? These may occur, especially in the early moments, when we're trying to learn how best to communicate with God.

How did Jonah know God's voice so well? Chances are, this wasn't the first time God had spoken to Jonah. It probably took years of really awkward moments before Jonah began to feel relaxed with God and feel like there was a solid relationship in place.

I remember playing a game when I was a teenager in youth group. One person was blindfolded, and everyone else used chairs to create an obstacle course through which the blindfolded person would attempt to navigate successfully. While I was blindfolded, my friends gathered around the obstacle course to shout out directions to me. One person would be secretly designated as the one to give correct directions while everyone else would yell out things that would lead me off track. It took trial and error, patience, lots of concentration, and some bruised shins, but eventually, I would figure out which voice to listen to and make it to the end of the course.

Learning to hear God's voice makes me think of that game. We recognize God's voice by determining which voices are not God's. Those are the voices that lead us into obstacles, rather than around them. Once we've determined which voices do not belong to God, we can become more in tune with God's calls to us.

Let's look more closely at this conversation between God and Jonah. Notice that God was not calling Jonah to devote his life to something. While God definitely does make these requests, in this instance Jonah was being called to complete one short task.

Don't misunderstand what I'm saying. God is just as powerful in these short tasks as in the life-long callings. The task that God was inviting Jonah to be a part of eventually would impact an entire city, not to mention millions who have read the story in the years since.

God's invitation to Jonah shows us something else very important about God. We can say, "No." Just like a child often says "no" to a parent, I have been guilty of saying the same thing to God many times in my life. I'm not proud of this. It's just a fact.

This does not mean that God will cease to pursue us. God pursued Jonah well after Jonah said, "No."

If we are not required to accept a call from God, then it only makes sense that God doesn't have to respond to our every desire! That is the basis of a relationship after all – when both parties exercise freely in the midst of the relationship.

If this is the case, why then was God so determined to ignore Jonah's response? In my way of thinking, the most obvious answer goes back to the relationship between a parent and child. If a child says, "No!" to eating peas, then a parent stereotypically responds back, "Eat your peas." The rationale being, in this imbalanced relationship, a parent knows best. By refusing a child's "no," a parent is attempting to forge healthier habits.

Perhaps God, the ultimate parent, is pursuing Jonah for this very reason. God knows that Jonah, who already does many things well, can grow even more and see the importance of answering the invitations God makes to him. Logically, this approach makes a lot of sense, but logic and life don't always agree.

The Logic of Jonah

God calls Jonah (1:2) = "Eat your peas!"

God pursues Jonah until Jonah gives in (1:4-3:3) = "Eat your peas or no dessert!"

God watches Jonah fulfill the appointed task with the desired results (3:4-3:10) = "See, the peas were not that bad, and they are good for you!"

God responds to all of Jonah's complaints (4:1-4:4) = "You are not going to die because you had to eat peas."

Still, Jonah is disgruntled (4:9) = "You ate the peas last week, why won't you eat them tonight?"

If the point of this entire exercise between God and

Jonah was for the "parent" to forge healthier habits in the "child," then it seems to have been an epic failure. It appears that Jonah's relationship with God grew worse as the story goes on.

However, Jonah's story is not over. It is kind of like watching the last episode of your favorite TV series and yelling at the TV, "It can't be the end!"

Wouldn't it be great to hear the full tale of what happens between God and Jonah after this story, to know of other times God pursues Jonah and to see how Jonah responds? We can take an educated guess, but wouldn't you love to know if Jonah learned his lesson once and for all?

This brief snapshot of Jonah's story is an invitation for us to learn more about what God's call looks like. While not responding affirmatively immediately after receiving God's call, we learn that it isn't the end of Jonah's story. From Jonah, we learn that our relationship with God is not defined by our failures, but by how we respond to them.

Let me suggest steps we can learn from Jonah regarding understanding God's call:

• First, a call from God will often include serving someone in need. Jonah was called, and responded so that the people of Nineveh might turn from their wickedness. Answering this type of call requires us to keep our eyes open so that we can see the needs around us. It comes in the form of a nudge on our heart that compels us to respond.

• Second, a call from God will invite you to grow as you step out into service. God calls each into service based on the gifts and talents that we have. God called Jonah because Jonah already had the gifts needed to go to Nineveh and be successful. There is something reassuring in God's method of calling us; God called Jonah to use gifts he already possessed, but also called on Jonah to grow during the process. Jonah could not remain the same. Think back on a time you responded to God's call. Did you grow from this experience?

• Finally, when you answer God's call, you will bear fruit! Jesus said that good trees would produce good fruit. In fact, you will recognize a good tree by its fruit. (Matthew 7:17-20)

When we respond to God's call, we live in connection with the ultimate good tree. When we respond affirmatively, we will produce good fruit. That's how we know we have answered a call from God – by our fruit. When Jonah finally answered "yes" to God's call, the results were obvious.

It's my hope that you never have to be eaten by a fish to respond to God's call. Nonetheless, we all stumble from time to time, but we serve a God who is an expert at picking us up and giving us more chances.

When you reflect upon times you have responded to God's call, can you remember good results from your efforts? Often the fruit can only be seen in hindsight. In some cases, we might never see it. Just the same, the fruit is there.

Learning to hear God's call is a process that takes effort, but it's a skill we can all develop. It requires reflecting – remembering calls from our past. It takes sharing, and listening to others share their experiences. Like many journeys, it requires attention, so that we can determine which voice is leading us in the right direction.

It is a journey that will lead us through failure and success. The goal is simply loving God with our whole heart, soul, and might. There will be obstacles, but trust God to lead you around them.

Reflection Questions

What voices, besides God's, are interfering with your
ability to recognize God's call when it comes?

Is there something you feel God is calling you to do right
now?

About the Authors

Julie Blackwelder Holly

Julie earned her Masters of Divinity from Duke Divinity School in 2004. Julie currently serves Birmingham-Southern College as Chaplain.

Wil Cantrell

Wil Cantrell serves on the staff of Concord United Methodist Church in Knoxville, Tennessee. Wil is a graduate of Duke Divinity School and author of ***Unafraid and Unashamed: Facing the Future of United Methodism.***"

Rob Couch

Rob Couch began his appointment as Lead Pastor of Christ United Methodist Church (Mobile, AL) on July 1, 2016. He received his Master of Divinity from Candler School of Theology and a Doctor of Ministry from Asbury Theological Seminary.

Bishop Robert Farr

Robert Farr serves as Bishop of the Missouri Area of The United Methodist Church. He has co-authored several books with Kay Kotan including: *Renovate or Die: 10 Ways to Focus Your Church in Mission*, *Get Their Name: Grow Your Church by Building New Relationships*, *10 Prescriptions for a Healthy Church*, and *The Necessary Nine*.

Aleze Fulbright

Aleze Fulbright currently serves the Indiana Conference as the Director of Leadership Development. She received her Masters in Divinity from Brite Divinity School at Texas Christian University. She also earned her Doctor of Ministry in Pastoral Leadership from Houston Graduate School of Theology.

Phil Maynard

Phil Maynard has served as Director of Path 1 Coaching Network, Excellence in Ministry Coaching, and Coach Training for Leaders. Phil is a graduate of Duke Divinity School (M.Div & Th.M); University of Kansas (M.S. Ed); and Drew (D.Min). He is author or co-author of several books, including his latest, *Discipler* (Market Square Books).

Larry Ousley

Dr. Larry Ousley recently retired as Executive Director of the Intentional Growth Center (IGC). Before coming to IGC in 2000, he served as senior pastor of several large churches in the Holston Conference of the UMC. Larry has lead approximately ten long-term group leadership coaching projects and has over 1,500 hours of experience coaching pastors, district superintendents, and conference staff persons.

Jacob Reedy

Jacob Reedy serves as associate pastor of Middlebrook Pike United Methodist Church in Knoxville, Tennessee. In addition to his work at Middlebrook Pike, Jacob serves on the Board of Directors of the Intentional Growth Center. He is a graduate of Methodist Theological School in Ohio.

Kevin Slimp

Kevin Slimp is publisher at Market Square Books. In previous careers, he has served as United Methodist youth pastor, national president of the United Methodist Youth Workers Association, and served on the extended cabinet of the Holston Conference of the UMC. These days, Kevin writes ... a lot. His most recent book is *The Good Folks of Lennox Valley.*

Bishop Debra Wallace-Padgett

Debra Wallace-Padgett currently serves as resident bishop of the Birmingham area of The United Methodist Church. At the time of her election at the 2012 Southeast Jurisdictional Conference, she served as Lead Pastor of St. Luke UMC in Lexington, Kentucky. She is a graduate of Scarritt College and Graduate School (M.A. in Christian Education), Lexington Theological Seminary (M. Div.) and Asbury Theological Seminary (D. Min.).

Other books from
Market Square Books

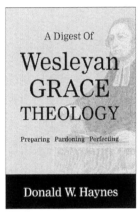

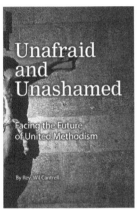

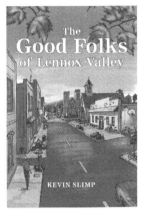

A Digest of
Wesleyan Grace Theology
Donald W. Haynes

Unafraid and Unashamed
Facing the Future of United Methodism
Wil Cantrell

The Good Folks
of Lennox Valley
Kevin Slimp

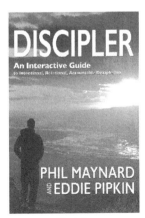

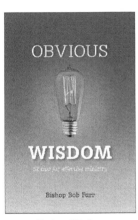

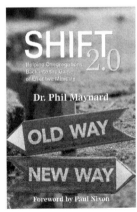

Discipler
An Interactive Guide
Phil Maynard and Eddie Pipkin

Obvious Wisdom
52 Tips for Effective Ministry
Bishop Robert Farr

Helping Congregations Shift 2
the Game of Effective Ministry
Phil Maynard

———— **marketsquarebooks.com** ————

"If you want the teens in your life to not only survive high school but thrive in it, while making their faith a priority, then they need this book!"

Rob Couch, Pastor, Christ United Methodist Church, Mobile AL

"Ashley shares her wisdom with a confident voice that no adult could ever use as effectively. I wish I had Ashley's Guide to Surviving High School to prepare me before my high school years."

Matthew Schiller, President, Catholic Press Association

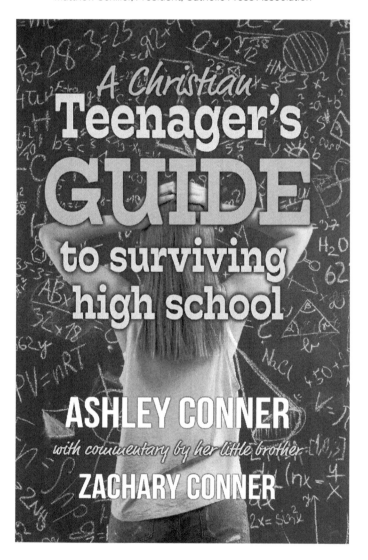

A Christian Teenager's GUIDE to surviving high school

ASHLEY CONNER

with commentary by her little brother

ZACHARY CONNER

Made in the USA
Middletown, DE
11 November 2018